Stories, Quips, and Quotes to Lift the Heart

hum♥R
for a friend's heart

Compiled by Shari MacDonald

Illustrated by Kristen Myers

HOWARD BOOKS
A DIVISION OF SIMON & SCHUSTER
New York   London   Toronto   Sydney

hum♥R
for the heart

Our purpose at Howard Books is to:
- *Increase faith* in the hearts of growing Christians
- *Inspire holiness* in the lives of believers
- *Instill hope* in the hearts of struggling people everywhere

Because He's coming again!

HOWARD
BOOKS

Published by Howard Books, a division of Simon & Schuster
1230 Avenue of the Americas, New York, NY 10020
www.howardpublishing.com

Humor for a Friend's Heart © 2005 by Howard Books

Library of Congress Cataloging-in-Publication Data
Humor for a friend's heart : stories, quips, and quotes to lift the heart / compiled by
Shari MacDonald ; illustrated by Kristen Myers.
   p. cm.
   ISBN 1-58229-428-3; ISBN 1-4165-3376-1
   1. American wit and humor. I. Myers, Kristen. II. Shari MacDonald.

PN6165.H84 2005
814'.608—dc22
                                                                2004059756

15 14 13 12 11 10 9 8 7

HOWARD is a registered trademark of Simon & Schuster, Inc.

Manufactured in the United States of America

For information regarding special discounts for bulk purchases, please contact Simon & Schuster Special Sales at 1-800-456-6798 or business@simonandschuster.com.

Compiled by Shari MacDonald
Cover art and illustrations by Kristen Myers
Cover design by LinDee Loveland
Interior design by Tennille Paden

Editorial Note: Mistakes in grammar and punctuation that were inherent in the original source were not corrected.

CONTENTS

Chapter 1: Friendship Means Never Having to Say You're Embarrassed

Funeral Friends—Phil Callaway..2

A Friendly Reminder—Rhonda Rhea...3

Burping to Bond—Karen Scalf Linamen 6

The Giddies—Tina Krause...9

Move Out!—Rhonda Rhea 11

Girlfriend Day '95—Cathy Lee Phillips 14

Love Me, Love My Mess—Tina Krause 18

Chapter 2: Friends Come in All Shapes and Sizes

The Best Kind of Friend—Barbara Johnson 22

The Spirit Is Willing, but the Dentures Are Missing
—Stan Toler 23

A Few Good Guys—Phil Callaway 25

Junior Friends—Barbara Johnson 29

Of Love and Friendship—Helen Widger Middlebrooke 33

Man's Best Friend—Brennan Manning 35

Shhh . . . Jesus Is in the Room—Cathy Lee Phillips 36

The Hug Is Sharper Than the Sword—G. Ron Darbee 41

Chapter 3: Of Friends and Kids

Heavenly Sermons—Cal and Rose Samra 48

You Know There's a Baby in the House When . . .
—Martha Bolton 49

Annual Letter—Lynn Bowen Walker 51

The Red Jell-O Caper—Barbara Johnson 53

Baby-U—Martha Bolton 56

I Once Was Lost—G. Ron Darbee 59

A-flat—Chris Ewing 66

Language Barriers—Martha Bolton 73

Chapter 4: Friends through It All

Old Friends—Martha Bolton 76

Friendship Is Blind—Charles Tindell 77

Girl Talk—Karen Scalf Linamen 78

With Nuts or Without?—Laura Jensen Walker 82

Make a Friend . . . Again—Karen Scalf Linamen 89

Sistership—Patsy Clairmont 92

With Friends like These—Luci Swindoll...........................95

Don't Look at Me—Tim Wildmon 96

Chapter 5: Real Men Do Have Friends

Golf Buddies—Phil Callaway 104

Craziness Loves Company—Phil Callaway 105

Geezer Guys—Dave Meurer 107

The Great Male Bonding Weekend—G. Ron Darbee 112

The Uncivil War—Dave Meurer 117

Tales of Mischief—Phil Callaway 122

Fishing Diary—Dave Meurer 126

Up in Smoke—Phil Callaway 130

Chapter 6: Friends: Can't Live without 'Em!

Complete Strangers—Lowell D. Streiker 136

There's No Friend like a Sister—Tina Krause 137

No Woman Is an Island—Karen Scalf Linamen 138

Planes, Trains, and Laughter—Luci Swindoll...........................142

Quack, Quack—Karen Scalf Linamen 144

Joy to the World—Susan Duke 149

Unexpected Delights—Luci Swindoll 158

There's Such a Thing as Too Much Encouragement
—Karen Scalf Linamen 161

Chapter 7: Friends You Can Count On

Two-Handed Friendship—Nigerian proverb......................................164

I've Only Got Eyelids for You—Martha Bolton...........................165

If I Should Die Before I Wake . . . Call My Friend
—Sue Buchanan...167

Death Doesn't Become Us—Martha Bolton..............................169

The Comfort of Friends—Barbara Johnson.............................171

Cornbread: The Stuff of Friendships—Cathy Lee Phillips.............172

Love in a Bear Suit—Susan Duke...175

Source Notes—183
Contributors—191

Friendship Means Never Having to Say You're Embarrassed

Funeral Friends

Elderly lady to a friend: "I will just die if nobody comes to my funeral."

—PHIL CALLAWAY
WHO PUT THE SKUNK IN THE TRUNK?

A Friendly Reminder

Rhonda Rhea

Friendships are a must for women. If it weren't for friends, women would have to go to the ladies' room alone. And who would offer a truthful assessment about whether an outfit makes your hips look big?

I have a Mustache Pact with my closest friends. If anyone of us goes into a coma, the others are honor bound by our pact to come and wax the mustache of the comatose friend. We women love to share those special moments.

I shared another special moment with friends recently. Several of us were hurrying to a surprise baby shower. We were hurrying because it's tough to surprise the guest of honor when she gets to the party before the guests.

We had pooled our resources to buy "the stroller to end all strollers." It was a collapsible stroller that would stroll the baby,

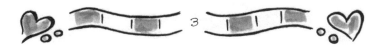

carry the baby, swing the baby—maybe even change the baby—I'm not sure. It was Stroller-ama.

I told the others to run in while I got Super Stroller. I jerked it into position and started sprinting. Unfortunately, about mid-driveway, Stroller-zilla realized I hadn't fully locked it into place (emphasis on the aforementioned collapsible feature). It collapsed neatly into storage mode.

I probably don't need to give you a science lesson on "momentum," but let me mention I had a lot of it working for me. The fact the Stroller-nator stopped on a dime didn't mean much to my little sprinting body, which was immediately airborne.

There are certain things, concepts, even certain words, only women understand.

Maybe you don't know me personally and think me ungraceful. Granted, you probably wouldn't want me to transport subatomic particles on a regular basis, but I don't want you to forever imagine me as a klutz. So maybe it would be better if you could please picture a graceful triple axel jump over the top of the stroller with sort of a one-point landing. I finished it off with a lovely flat-on-the-back pose, staring up at the sky for effect. I'd give it a 6.9.

Thankfully, I had my wonderful friends there to rush over and make sure I was okay. Of course, they couldn't actually ask me if I was all right since those dear friends were laughing so hard they were about to damage some internal organs! One of them couldn't even stay. She made a beeline for the house. You know what can happen to laughing mothers.

That's another thing we love to share: laughter.

This is a little reminder. If it's been awhile since you've made time for friends, take the time and share a laugh with a sister. We need each other. There are certain things, concepts, even certain words, only women understand. "Mauve" and "taupe" are a couple of good examples.

Call up your special bud today. While you have her on the line, you might also want to take care of that coma/mustache thing.

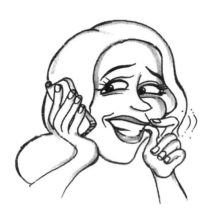

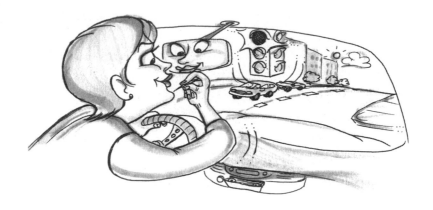

Burping to Bond
Karen Scalf Linamen

There are lots of maladies common to women.

I got an e-mail the other day from a reader who wrote, "I loved your story about keeping your tweezers in the car and plucking chin hairs at stop lights. I thought I was the only woman who did that! I also use my mascara to cover up my gray roots between hair colorings. But don't let it smudge. It's a mess!"

See? That's one of the things I love about being a woman. We may share common maladies, but we're also willing to share a good solution when we find one.

Last week I took Kacie to the park near my house. While she tackled the rope ladder, I introduced myself to a couple other moms there with their kids.

Within five minutes we were exchanging bladder control stories.

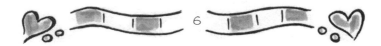

Honestly, I don't know how I get myself into these kinds of conversations with women I've known all of seven minutes, but this is not an unusual experience for me.

We blamed our pregnancies, of course, and then traded secrets about Kegels and other exercises, as well as which maxi-pads to wear when attending high-risk events such as Chonda Pierce concerts.

It was amazing what we all had in common.

And don't even get me started on what babies and birthdays do to our breasts.

I've always wanted to take up jogging, but my time has passed. I might have gotten away with it in my twenties, but these days I'd not only come home with shin splints but black eyes as well.

When I was a teenager the burning question in my mind was, Who am I and what is my significance in this world?

In my twenties I wondered, How can I have an impact in my career, community, and family?

In my thirties I asked, How can I leave this world a better place for my children?

Now that I'm forty what I *really* want to know is, Where do my breasts go when I lay down?

Remember that song we learned as kids? The words went, "Do your ears hang low, do they wobble to and fro? Can you tie them in a knot? Can you tie them in a bow?" When I was eleven I thought it was hilarious to sing about feminine body parts other than ears. I had no idea one day it would come true.

The Bible says there's nothing new under the sun. This is one of the reasons I know other women deal with the same questions

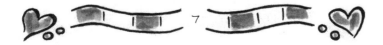

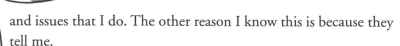

and issues that I do. The other reason I know this is because they tell me.

Women talk to each other about these things. I don't know if men dig deep into their souls for these kinds of intimate confessions when they get together, but I have my doubts. My friend Beth says sometimes she eavesdrops on her teenage son when he's on the phone with his friends. She says teenage boys can be on the phone for hours and exchange less than nine words in the process.

I asked, "So what are they doing?"

She tilted her head, trying to remember. "Oh, I don't know. Burping mostly."

Which, now that I think about it, seems a far more intimate exchange than the mere telling of bladder stories.

Maybe they're onto something after all.

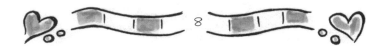

The Giddies
Tina Krause

Single file, I followed the other choir members to the choir loft. The organ accompanied our procession, robes swaying with each step. Church was about to begin, so I put forth an effort to look my Sunday best.

But I had one problem. Before the service, another choir member and I had engaged in some lighthearted jesting. Now we had a serious case of the giddies. Everything struck a humorous chord—the pastor's slight hop to the platform, the choir director's mannerisms, and the child squirming in the front pew.

Facing the congregation, I tried to restrain my laughter as my face flushed and tears formed. Church members peered over the tops of their hymnals looking at me. For a moment I was fine until I noticed a fly land on Mrs. Baker's head. She swatted the pest; then it landed on her face. She flinched and shooed it away, but it landed again. Her eyebrows furrowed as she stared at the

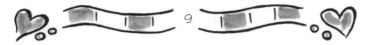

pest, waiting for it to take flight. When it did, she waved her hands like a flagman at an Indy 500 race.

Instantly, my shoulders shook as laughter bubbled within like a volcano about to erupt. My friend alongside of me put her hand over her mouth and stared at the floor. Meanwhile, I prayed that I could gain control.

All eyes were on the front. *Quick, think sad thoughts,* I told myself in desperation—anything to cure the giggles. But nothing worked. The minister's mispronunciation of a name set me off again as waves of unrestrained chuckles rippled from my mouth.

Finally, the worst—an unexpected snort. Eyebrows lifted with frowns of disapproval. I wanted to disappear. *How could I allow myself to get so out of control? What must everyone think? What must the pastor think? What must* God *think?*

In an instant, the giddies vanished while humiliation and embarrassment gripped me like two giant bear claws. I bowed my head, my face now flushed for a different reason.

To my relief, the pastor whisked around and quipped, "If a merry heart works like a medicine as the Scriptures say, someone in the choir is the healthiest person in here!"

Laughter filled the sanctuary and I was comforted. My pastor's gracious lightheartedness rescued me.

Most of us go to church dressed in our Sunday clothes and Sunday smiles. We want folks to applaud our spirituality. But occasionally something occurs to expose what we really are: human.

When our human frailties break through in waves of the ridiculous, God's mercy prevails. After all, to be human isn't a sin, but to pretend we're not is really something to laugh about!

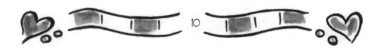

Move Out!

Rhonda Rhea

"Move out" takes on a truly military tone when seven years' worth of junk has to be stuffed into seven thousand cardboard boxes. Factor in my five pack-rat kids and you understand these were no ordinary moving maneuvers. I wondered how on earth I could relocate without a backhoe. This was a major battle.

You should've seen me on packing day. I paced back and forth in front of the ladies who had come to help. I was the commander, readying the troops. My feather duster was tucked under my arm like a riding crop as I began my moving address: "I'd like to thank you for signing on for this mission. Some of you might find yourselves waning in the heat of the battle. Others may discover new courage. And some of you . . . (sniff) . . . might not be coming home."

Okay, that was for drama. They all made it home. Not without battle scars, however. It was frightening; I didn't have mere

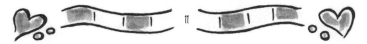

dust bunnies on top of my china cabinet. These things looked more like fuzzy buffaloes.

Thankfully, I had provided the women with some basic training. I decided I could desensitize them before they got to the house by taking them for a ride in my minivan. On the way to my buffalo-filled home, one asked, "Is this a pickle in the cup holder?"

"My kids don't eat pickles. I think that's a hotdog from last baseball season." She had to go home right after she regained consciousness. The rest of the ladies were fine after they put their heads between their knees. Still, I couldn't bring myself to make them look in the glove compartment. I think the Geneva Convention has rules against such atrocities.

I couldn't bring myself to make them look in the glove compartment.

Several were overcome during the chemical warfare phase of the moving battle. It's a common result of mixing the chemicals needed to fight dust buffaloes with the ones needed for that scum that gathers over the stove. They're recovering. The therapy for post-packing trauma syndrome (PPTS) is also helping. Thankfully, the flashbacks are starting to subside.

There was a particularly perilous moment in the kitchen, however, when one of the ladies made a gruesome discovery. It was a potato that had fallen behind a pile of junk in one of the cabinets. But it was no longer legally a potato. It looked like a brown, raisiney grenade. We were all distressed when we discovered the local bomb squad doesn't respond to potatoes.

I was amazed no one in my family had ever gotten a whiff of the rotting potato/grenade. We never had even a hint it was back there shriveling. Believe it or not, there wasn't even any mold on the little sucker. I guess it's still not surprising not one of the packing ladies wanted to touch the thing. But before we could move, the dead spud had to go.

In the same way, isn't it amazing the spiritual dirt we can have hidden away? Little things can be rotting—shriveling right under our noses—and we don't so much as catch a whiff. It's a spiritual battle and the enemy is ever ready to lob his bombs. He loves to see us rendered fruitless. Sometimes he schemes a sneak attack. It's not the kind of attack that immediately blows up in our faces, but rather an undercover mission where the enemy secures hidden places of rottenness that quietly shrivel our spirits.

Romans 6:13 says, "Do not offer the parts of your body to sin, as instruments of wickedness, but rather offer yourselves to God, as those who have been brought from death to life." We can ignore those pockets of disobedience we've tucked away, or we can offer every part of ourselves to God. Before we can move to a closer walk with Him, we shouldn't be surprised if He pulls out that "sin potato" and says, "We really have to take care of this before we can move on."

I've now moved into a clean, new home—completely free of shriveled potatoes. When we allow the Father to cleanse us from sneaky rottenness, we can enjoy the same kind of clean, sweet closeness with Him.

So go ahead. Plan a spiritual military action of your own. Execute Recon Plan "Tossoutthepotato!" Ready? Move out!

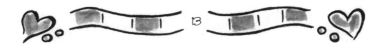

Girlfriend Day '95

Cathy Lee Phillips

So, I suppose you are wondering, "What is Girlfriend Day?"

Simply stated, it is an annual outing celebrating friendship. Of course, I realize that most people spend special time with friends, but Girlfriend Day is unique and characterized by certain essential elements.

First, you obviously need a friend. Jennifer Huycke is my choice for this annual outing. Next, you need a day with no other obligations (good luck finding this!).

Once these basic requirements have been met, the fun begins—shopping, lunching, laughing, and talking. You know, girlfriend things. Oh, and I almost forgot . . . chocolate! I do realize, of course, that men would probably prefer something along the lines of fishing, golfing, and beef jerky. Our version of Girlfriend Day certainly does not include beef jerky—only the girl things mentioned above.

Without a doubt, Girlfriend Day '95 has been the most memorable so far for Jennifer and me. It began harmlessly enough. Jennifer and I spent the morning in the mall where the shopping was plentiful—and so was the chocolate. We lunched at Olive Garden then wandered among the shops across the street from the mall.

Though we are best friends, Jennifer and I have very different tastes in clothing. I like beautiful floral designs. Jennifer likes weird geometric shapes. I prefer soothing pink and blue pastels. Jennifer goes for bright primary colors. Though we might enter a store together, we quickly go to our separate corners and the game begins. We grab sweaters, pants, shirts, and dresses. We grab almost anything off the "For Sale" rack. And if a "Clearance" sign is anywhere within the store, it's a feeding frenzy. To be honest, Jennifer has been known to chase flashing blue lights from one corner of K-Mart to the other. In fact, the blue light on a passing police car causes her body to immediately secrete large quantities of shopping hormones.

Very little conversation is required during the Girlfriend Day shopping free-for-all. Therefore, store employees rarely know we are shopping together, let alone celebrating an annual event.

In one store, however, Jennifer asked my opinion regarding a sweater she found. It was beautiful—not at all what I expected her to select. The background was a soft ivory and it was adorned with petite flowers and designs embroidered in pale pinks and greens. The good news was that it was on sale. The bad news was that it was missing one of the pearl buttons that adorned the front of the sweater. The missing button was in a very obvious place and was so unique we knew the odds of finding a match were not good.

"Maybe they have a spare button," I suggested.

"Or maybe they will give me another $10 off the price," Jennifer responded. (Yes, she is my best friend but, quite frankly, Jennifer can be really cheap at times).

We walked to the cashier, each holding a pile of clothing to purchase. Jennifer, of course, was quick to mention the missing button. From beneath the counter the cashier pulled a box containing buttons of every size, shape, and color imaginable. Alas, no match was to be found.

The cashier was obviously going to grant her request. It was then that the devil just grabbed hold of me.

Smelling blood, Jennifer moved in for the kill.

"Well, is it possible to have the sweater at a reduced price since we cannot find the matching button?" Jennifer asked so sweetly.

The cashier was obviously going to grant her request. It was then that, I suppose, the devil just grabbed hold of me.

"Excuse me, ma'am," I spoke to the cashier in my most self-righteous voice, "but I cannot remain silent. (Can you just feel the drama?) I must tell you I saw this woman rip the button off that sweater."

Dead silence.

Not realizing we were actually friends celebrating Girlfriend Day '95, the cashier stuttered and stammered, obviously not knowing what to do or say. After a moment, however, Jennifer became quite vocal.

"You lie!" she suddenly shrieked, her eyes wide with surprise. "You must die!"

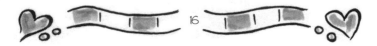

Sweat popped out on the brow of the cashier. She must have feared a rumble right there in the middle of Fashion Bug.

"I'm sorry," I replied innocently, "but I've never seen this woman before in my life."

By this time I was becoming concerned about Jennifer's red face and blood pressure. Her shock quickly turned to laughter and our nervous cashier finally realized this was an innocent joke between two good friends. This innocent cashier even laughed with us. All three of us held our sides as tears ran down our faces. We explained our annual outing to the frazzled cashier who thought Girlfriend Day was a grand idea.

We all decided that moment would obviously be the highlight of Girlfriend Day '95.

The button was never found. Jennifer did buy her sweater at a $10 reduced price. The cashier was still laughing as we left. And I'll never forget her parting words.

"A friendship like yours is a real blessing from heaven."

"Yes ma'am, it is. It really is."

Love Me, Love My Mess
Tina Krause

I'm staring at the interior of my car, alias the roving catchall chamber of my life. It's the holding station for junk mail (that usually slips between the seats), a crushed Kleenex box, an empty Tic-Tac container, loose coins, and numerous crumpled napkins that I use to write notes on. The glove compartment brims with some very old ketchup and salt packets, bent straws, and a few indiscriminate grease-stained receipts from all those clandestine trips to McDonald's. And there's that clothes hanger left over from the time I stopped at a gas station to change from casual clothes into something dressier on my way to a baby shower.

I'd rather eat worms than allow the inside of my house to resemble anything close to the interior of my car. But for some reason sloppiness is acceptable behavior within the four doors of my comfortable—albeit unkempt—Dodge Shadow.

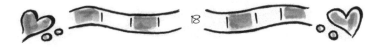

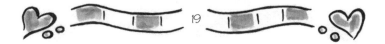

Recently, I drove my friend on an errand. As she entered my catchall chamber, I unfurled apologies, tossing and jostling items out of her way with giant heaves. "Oops, sorry about that," I blathered after she, despite my efforts, snagged her nylons on the clothes hanger when she pushed aside the crumpled napkins to find a seat.

"I don't get it," she said with a puzzled expression. "Your house is so spotless, but your car . . ."

There is no logical explanation. Nor can I explain why the inside of my purse resembles a war zone while the inside of my cabinets would charm the executive editor of *Better Homes and Gardens.*

Human behavior seldom makes sense. I've encountered tight-wads who shudder at spending a few cents for a cup of coffee but blow thousands of greenbacks on sports cars or large screen TVs. Asked to donate a few dollars to the Lord's work and they break into a cold sweat. Yet they are the first in line to buy Lotto tickets at the convenience store.

Likewise, I sometimes think I know who I am, but my actions contradict me. I guess God is the sole discerner of hearts. Which makes me wonder: am I really sure that I possess genuine organizational and meticulous housekeeping tendencies? After all, how confident can one be whose car resembles a nomadic dumpsite?

"You know, I may be a bag lady just waiting to emerge," I said to my friend as we cruised down the street, knee high in debris.

She studied my face, expressionless.

"Did you hear me?" I probed.

"Yep, I heard you."

"Well?"

Almost missing a stop sign, I slammed on the brakes, and like a meteor shower, the pennies I stashed on the dashboard flung themselves toward her. "You might be right," she replied, dodging the spray. "Yes, I'm sure you're right."

Spiritually as well, I often have more adjustments to make than I'm willing to admit. But with God's assistance, a transformation is possible even in the most remote catchall chambers of my heart, where He alone is able to tackle the debris.

What's more—unlike some of my car's passengers—He's unafraid of what He'll find once inside.

Friends Come in All Shapes and Sizes

The Best Kind of Friend

Life would be much easier if you only had fat friends.

—BARBARA JOHNSON
FRESH ELASTIC FOR STRETCHED OUT MOMS

The Spirit Is Willing, but the Dentures Are Missing

Stan Toler

Grandpa and Grandma were sitting in their porch rockers, watching the beautiful sunset and reminiscing about "the good old days," when Grandma turned to Grandpa and said, "Honey, do you remember when we first started dating and you used to just casually reach over and take my hand?"

Grandpa looked over at her, smiled, and took her aged hand in his.

With a wry little smile, Grandma pressed a little further, "Honey, do you remember how, after we were engaged, you'd sometimes lean over and suddenly kiss me on the cheek?"

Grandpa leaned slowly toward Grandma and gave her a lingering kiss on her wrinkled cheek.

Growing bolder still, Grandma said, "Honey, do you remember how, after we were first married, you'd nibble on my ear?"

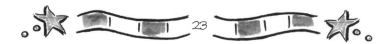

Grandpa slowly got up from his rocker and headed into the house. Alarmed, Grandma said, "Honey, where are you going?" Grandpa replied, "To get my teeth!"

A Few Good Guys

Phil Callaway

A few years ago, I began to realize that many of those I considered my best friends had moved far away, and if things were going to change, I would have to change them. So one morning I asked a new friend out for coffee and popped the question. "Hey," I said, past a mouthful of muffin, "how about we get some guys together a few times a month for a reading group? We'll discuss something serious, like Plato . . . or Archie. We can meet at my house."

The idea was met with a stifled yawn. "Phil," he said, "I'm busier than a wasp at a barbecue. Besides, a reading club sounds about as exciting as watching cheese mold."

"Well," I stammered, "how about we . . . uh . . . how about we get together and just eat. Ya, that's it. An eating club. We'll sample desserts, then have a lively discussion to burn off the calories."

"Now you're talking," said my new friend, squeezing the creamer way too hard. "Sorry about that . . . here's a napkin."

It's been four years since I cleaned that shirt. Four years since the Circle of Six began convening almost every other Tuesday. For reasons of international security, I can't say much, but I will tell you that each member has agreed to adhere to some strict guidelines as laid out in our red Principles and Procedures notebook:

Rule #1: Be there at 8:30 p.m. Unless you're late.

Rule #2: Hosts will be selected in alphabetical sequence. If you are hosting the event, bake something. We reserve the right to watch you eat it first. If you choke, lose consciousness, or die, we will try to revive you. We will not, however, eat your baking.

Rule #3: If you bring a cell phone, we will take it apart and hide the pieces.

Rule #4: No talking about Amway or Mannatech. Unless you have a really good story about someone who sells it.

Rule #5: The food must be better than last time we were at your house. If this means your wife bakes it, that's okay. No, your wife may not attend the meeting.

Rule #6: When we run out of food and things to say, the assembly is adjourned.

Tonight we're meeting by candlelight for my wife's cheesecake. It is available in three flavors: Strawberry Slam, Triple Raspberry Rage, and Death by Chocolate. Helpings come in three sizes—the Ballerina, the Allegro, and the Cardiac Arrest. Collectively, we have gained more than 100 pounds in four years of Tuesdays. None of us quite knows why. We've also gained some friends. I wish you could meet these guys. A nicer bunch you're unlikely to find. A better-looking, wealthier bunch, perhaps. But these are the kind of friends you'd crawl through a minefield for. If I were

heading into battle, well, I would take some Marines. But I'd want these guys to bring the cheesecake.

When I think of real guys, I think of Vance, Ron, Harold, James, and Glenn. And I think of the following characteristics:

Graceful. You should see these guys swoop down on a dessert. Such speed, grace, and elegance is seldom glimpsed outside ballet halls. But they are also full of grace when it comes to conversation. This is not Gossip 101. This is Sinners Anonymous. Overwhelmed by God's grace, we are looking for ways to pass it on. We do not spend our evenings pointing out the shortcomings of others, because we have encountered a few of our own. We also know that when you point a finger, four fingers are pointing toward you.

Understanding. Though we have come frighteningly close to tears on two occasions, if you come here looking for hugs and sensitivity, you may be disappointed. But if you're looking for some timely advice, or a listening ear, it's great to be surrounded by a few wise guys. In the Psalms, David prays often for

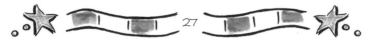

Collectively, we have gained more than 100 pounds in four years of Tuesdays.

understanding. In Psalm 119:34, he asks God, "Give me understanding, and I will keep your law and obey it with all my heart."

Yielded. We sometimes disagree on child rearing or music or automobile brands. But we share one thing in common. Each of us has handed the steering wheel over to God. Yes, we sometimes want to take it back or offer suggestions on how to drive. But we're learning. Together.

Successful. Tonight we got to talking about Stuff we wish we had. About riding lawn mowers, and power sprayers, and hot tubs. Then we laughed. Though it's easy to forget, success is not defined by the stuff we grab, but by the footprints we leave. Our incomes don't define success. Our legacy does.

It was slow going at first. Guys aren't always comfortable talking about what's really happening in our lives. We hide behind the weather and the New York Yankees. But before long someone removes his catcher's mask and admits that he's just an old sinner in need of God's grace. And before you know it the clock strikes midnight and you're all sitting around wishing it hadn't.

Tonight we talk about a friend's failed marriage and what it takes to keep the flame burning. After we say goodnight, I sit on the sofa wishing that every guy on earth had this many friends. Guys who love to laugh. Guys who know that burdens are lighter and the path a whole lot brighter when traveled with a few fat friends.

Now, it's time to clean the candle wax off my wife's tablecloth. And, oh yes, I need to do something with this last piece of cheesecake.

Junior Friends

Barbara Johnson

I have learned to find fun in unlikely places. Fun is a mystery. You cannot trap it like an animal; you cannot catch it like the flu. But it comes without bidding, if you are looking for it.

Recently I made a trip—by plane to Michigan for the funeral of a beloved aunt. As I boarded my return flight to California, I noticed a little girl, sitting all hunched up across the aisle from me. She looked so small and so afraid. The flight attendant told me she was traveling alone.

I thought, *Oh, well, the attendants will look after her.* I was busy going over the last few days . . . the funeral . . . the many people who had grown older since I had last seen them . . . It was all very depressing. I knew the five-hour flight home would be my only time to be alone with my loss. I had no intention of entertaining a little six-year-old who evidently had never been on a plane before.

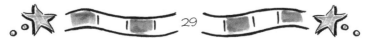

As the plane took off, I noticed that she shut her eyes tightly and clenched the seat belt with bone-white knuckles. I felt something inside me want to ask her to come sit by me.

When we were safely in the air, I asked the attendant if it was all right, and she replied, "Oh, yes! She has never flown before. Her parents have divorced, and she's on her way to California to live with relatives she's never even met before. Thank you for caring."

My "fun" started when the hostess came through with the complimentary beverages. Darling little Suzie with her dancing black eyes said she would have a 7-Up. I asked the hostess to put it in a fancy glass, with a cherry in it, because we were pretending we were special VIP ladies taking a super trip. Having 7-Up with a cherry in it in a fancy glass may not be your idea of fun, but to a six-year-old who had never had it that way before, it was great fun. We were off to a great start.

> I noticed that she shut her eyes tightly and clenched the seat belt with bone-white knuckles.

Our pretending went on, and I could see that I had missed so much in having all boys, never learning as a mother of a girl what little girls thought of. Suzie thought the luncheon on the plane was just like miniatureland. The tiny salt containers were a great joke. The tiny cup from the salad dressing was just for Munchkins. I had so much fun, enjoying with her child's eyes, all the goodies on our trays. We had our own special tea party. The little paper umbrella anchored in the dessert caused her to remark, "I got to see *Mary Poppins* once." I knew this was one of her most special experiences, and so we pre-

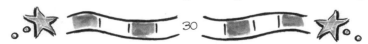

tended that she was Mary Poppins. We kept her little umbrella, and Suzie had to learn to walk like Mary Poppins, with her toes sideways and holding the umbrella up just so. She did a great imitation!

Just taking Suzie to the little bathroom was an experience. She couldn't figure out how things worked. She wanted to know if the soap was small because somebody had used it almost all up!

When we returned to our seats, the attendant gave us both coloring books and three crayons—blue, red, and yellow. So, together, we colored some puppies in the book red, made a yellow gypsy, and a blue ballerina. It was fun! She had lost her fear of flying, and we looked out on the cottony sea of clouds, talking about what fun it would be to walk on the clouds, holding our Mary Poppins umbrellas, and see how far we could go.

Then it was time to land. The hours had melted away. I had been a child for a few hours, playing her game, coloring her pictures, exploring her child's mind, seeing life through the eyes of a six-year-old. I had learned so much!

I will always remember that fun day, and when I eat on an airline flight, I always think of the "Munchkin" dinner Suzie and I shared that day. She got off ahead of me when we landed, and I rushed to try to catch up with her. I saw as she was swooped up into the arms of a grandmotherly lady with twinkles in her eyes. Suzie turned to me and said, "Look, Grandma, I am Mary Poppins!" She held her little umbrella up, turned her little feet sideways, and smiled a big smile of pure joy. The grandmother thanked me for looking after her, but *I* was the one who was taken care of that day!

It could have been a dreary, sad trip for me, lost in my own

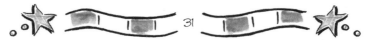

reverie of sorrow, but instead a little girl became a diamond of love and joy for me.

When life gets so heavy for you, and you wonder how you can cope with all the load, learn to put on the garment of joy for the spirit of heaviness, and fun is included in that garment of joy. Suzie turned my desert into a decorated place of joy. Look for that joy in your life, too. Don't settle for grouchiness and sorrow: settle for joy and happiness.

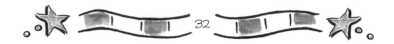

Of Love and Friendship

Helen Widger Middlebrooke

Matthew and Sally had been buddies since she had arrived in New York that summer. Sally was the best pal a boy could have—she ran, climbed, and drove a mean Big Wheel. She played so rough that I doubted Matthew thought of Sally as a girl.

But one December day before Sally's birthday, I found out otherwise.

As we drove by the turnoff to Sally's house, Matthew stared down the street. "I want to get Sally a birthday present," he declared.

No problem, I thought. Footballs were easy to find.

"What do you want to get her?"

"A dress."

I nearly wrecked the van. "*Really?* A dress?"

"Yes. I want to get her a pretty dress. She needs a pretty dress."

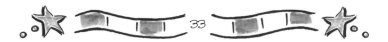

In the following days, I tried to dissuade him. I wasn't ready to be Casanova's mother. But his desire grew; by the time we got to the thrift store, he was hunting for a "pretty silver dress that shined in the sunlight."

There were no silver dresses, but he was undaunted. Like a Fifth Avenue merchandiser, he compared styles and stitching. Heart-shaped buttons, nice. Had a spot, no good.

I watched in amazement. I was rearing a sensitive nineties guy. I wasn't ready.

He settled on a red print dress with white trim, three-quarter-length sleeves, and dropped waistline.

We washed and wrapped the treasured dress. He made a card: "Dear Sally, I hope you have a happy birthday. I hope you like my present."

Sally wore the dress to church the next day. It fit perfectly. And while it didn't shine, Sally did.

And Matthew did, too.

That was six years ago. The dress is in my attic. Sally lives in Illinois and has outgrown tomboyhood.

And Matthew has met another athletic girl with the same birthday.

Last week he was at it again, shopping for something silver or shiny. He found jewelry.

Someday, it's going to be diamonds.

And I'm not going to be ready.

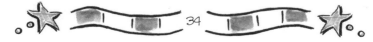

Man's Best Friend

Brennan Manning

The story is told of a man who went to the priest and said, "Father, I want you to say a Mass for my dog."

The priest was indignant. "What do you mean, say a Mass for your dog?"

"It's my pet dog," said the man. "I loved that dog and I'd like you to offer a Mass for him."

"We don't offer Masses for dogs here," the priest said. "You might try the denomination down the street. Ask them if they have a service for you."

As the man was leaving, he said to the priest. "I really loved that dog. I was planning to offer a million-dollar stipend for the Mass."

And the priest said, "Wait a minute. You never told me your dog was Catholic."

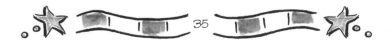

Shhh...Jesus Is in the Room
Cathy Lee Phillips

Six first-grade teachers at Garrett Elementary School held their breaths and glanced nervously about the room. They were receiving the list of children they would educate, guide, and discipline for the coming school year. They were friends and colleagues who wished no hardship on anyone, but each secretly prayed, "Please, Lord, give him to another teacher."

After taking kindergarten by storm, Jason Montgomery was entering the first grade. In his wake, he left behind one distraught kindergarten teacher (still in therapy), one troubled paraprofessional, and one weary principal who knew the child and his parents on a first-name basis. He also had all their phone numbers committed to memory. Jason Montgomery was talkative, hyperactive, and an ingenious troublemaker. He defied adults, intimidated classmates, and cast fear into the hearts of those teachers who waited anxiously to learn which of them

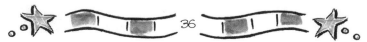

would be Jason Montgomery's next target. The sheets were distributed and, almost immediately, a dreadful wail arose from the back left corner of the room. Mrs. Donovan, a seasoned veteran who had taught first grade for well over a decade, appeared catatonic, her student list clenched tightly in her right hand.

The principal broke the silence.

"Don't worry, Mrs. Donovan, your therapy will be covered by our Worker's Comp Insurance."

The family of teachers at Garrett Elementary School gathered around to offer support, but Mrs. Donovan took a deep breath and vowed not to be driven to despair by Jason Montgomery. For the next three days, she concentrated on decorating and preparing her classroom for the onslaught of students who would soon be arriving. Her final chore was to place a name board on the wall—a big blue poster listing the name of every child in her class.

A varied collection of first-graders and parents entered her room the next morning and Mrs. Donovan greeted all with her typical smile. She trembled slightly when she spotted Jason Montgomery accompanied by his mother. Looking somewhat battered and fatigued, Mrs. Montgomery seemed practically joyful when she left her son in the capable hands of his new teacher. She returned to her car and prayed for Jason's conduct and Mrs. Donovan's nerves. Relishing the golden silence inside the car, she drove home, wondering just how soon it would be before the principal would call with details of Jason's latest disruption.

Meanwhile, Mrs. Donovan greeted her students.

"I want to learn your names so I have made name tags for each of you to wear today. Please sit very still while I place the name tag on your shirt."

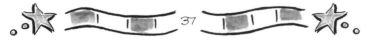

Everyone, including Jason Montgomery, obeyed.

Then Mrs. Donovan pointed to the big blue poster on the wall.

"Boys and girls, this is a list of all your new friends. While I learn your names, I want you to learn the names of all the other boys and girls in our class."

The name of every student was listed in alphabetical order on the big blue name board.

Mrs. Donovan then talked about school rules, read a book, and taught her students a new song, all the while keeping Jason Montgomery under constant surveillance. But Jason never caused a problem. To her surprise, he never talked out of turn, wandered around the room, or insulted the other students.

Was this the real Jason Montgomery? The teacher could not comprehend Jason's behavior. Neither did the principal. Neither did the other first-grade teachers who took turns checking on Mrs. Donovan throughout the day. And neither did Mrs. Montgomery when she picked Jason up at the end of the day.

"I knew it would not last," Jason's mother thought. "Here comes the bad news."

"Jason was a good boy?" his mother asked suspiciously.

"A perfect angel."

Although Mrs. Montgomery praised Jason for his astonishing behavior, she was certain it would not continue.

But it did continue—through the first week, the first month, and the first six weeks of the school year. There were no phone calls from a frantic principal and no notes from a beleaguered teacher. Unbelievable!

As the seventh week began, Mrs. Donovan called Mrs. Montgomery for a parent-teacher conference.

"Please bring Jason along," Mrs. Donovan requested.

"I knew it would not last," Jason's mother thought. "Here comes the bad news."

Not so. Mrs. Donovan simply wanted to praise and congratulate Jason in the presence of his mother.

Astounded, Jason's mother could no longer keep quiet. Leaning toward her son, she asked, "Honey, you have been such a good boy this year and I am very proud of you. But why have you been so good this year when you were always in trouble last year?"

Jason raised his blue eyes and simply said, "Jesus is in my room."

"Yes, Jason, we believe Jesus is everywhere, but . . ."

"But, Mommy, Jesus really is in my room. Look!"

Jason pointed to the big blue name board that alphabetically listed the students in Mrs. Donovan's class.

Garrett Elementary School had a variety of students, many of whom were Hispanic, including Jesus Alvarez who was listed first on the big blue name board. Though Jason had not learned a lot of words, he certainly recognized the name of JESUS when he saw it.

Jason's mother and teacher could barely contain their laughter.

"Oh, Jason, let me explain. You see . . ."

Clearing her throat and interrupting, the wise first-grade teacher spoke, "Mrs. Montgomery, we really do not need to confuse Jason with a lot of unnecessary details, do we?" Mrs. Donovan obviously knew a good thing when she saw one.

"You are right, Mrs. Donovan. Thank you. I just hope Jason will always have Jesus in his room."

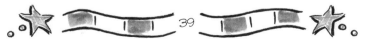

"Amen to that." His teacher smiled. "Amen to that."

What about you? Been misbehaving? You had better straighten up and be on your best behavior. Admit it—Jesus is in the room.

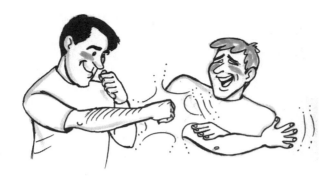

The Hug Is Sharper Than the Sword

G. Ron Darbee

One thing I have noticed over the years is that the masculine world is divided into two distinct camps: those who hug and those who hug not. Due to what I attribute, in part, to too many years of barracks life and more than my fair share of gym locker rooms, I cast my lot unreservedly with the latter crowd and let the chips fall where they may.

In this age of sensitivity and self-examination, guys like me are beginning to get a bad rap for our reluctance to embrace our fellow man. Critics (die-hard, groping huggers) accuse us of every character flaw from harboring fears of intimacy to homophobic anxiety. Neither is the case, of course. We, the unhuggable masses, simply choose to display affection in other, more definitively masculine ways.

Traditionally, men have always felt more comfortable expressing their feelings for one another in forums where masculinity is

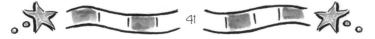

left unquestioned—the playing field or locker room, for example. Nothing says "I love you, Man," like the crisp snap of a wet towel in the small of your buddy's back. A sharp jab to the shoulder also shows you care, though prudence suggests developing more than a passing acquaintance prior to exercising a serious shoulder jab. Some guys consider a pat on the backside acceptable, but only if delivered by a member of the coaching staff, and even then some fairly strict guidelines apply.

In an attempt to assist my fellow man, particularly men who share my fear of the awkwardness brought about by physical intimacy, I have endeavored to categorize the various hugging classifications. This information should be guarded closely, lest it fall into the wrong hands and ultimately be turned against us. If studied earnestly and properly applied, this data will empower you to quickly and easily recognize high hug-risk conditions, and apply appropriate countermeasures.

The Compulsive Hugger

Probably the easiest of the squeeze-happy persuasion to identify, the compulsive hugger finds it impossible to exercise any self-control in social situations. This individual lives to hug and believes that he must grab somebody—anybody—upon entering a room. Once spotted and, if possible, tagged for tracking and future identification, the compulsive hugger proves the easiest to avoid, since you know what to expect and can easily escape an embarrassing situation.

One important point to note: occasionally, you may come in contact with a compulsive hugger of the large and muscular variety. In this case, simply accept the gesture in the nature it was intended. There is no sense in offending large, muscular

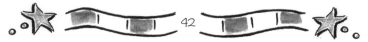

men, especially when they have their arms wrapped securely around you.

The Emotional Hugger

Emotional huggers may go completely unnoticed until such time when they are particularly moved or overcome with sentiment (Superbowl Sunday or game seven of the World Series, for instance). Understandably taken with the momentous occasion at hand, the emotional hugger immediately gropes around for a victim to bond with and share his experience.

The Malicious Hugger

Hard as it is to believe, some men actually enjoy hugging other men for the sheer satisfaction they derive in catching us off-guard. These men are often of the large, muscular variety and know they can get away with the affront. The best defense when faced with a malicious hugger is to smile, return the gesture, and hope you spoil his fun enough to send him seeking another victim elsewhere.

Nothing says "I love you, Man," like the crisp snap of a wet towel in the small of your buddy's back.

As an active member of a large, growing church, I run across the full spectrum of men on any given Sunday. Conscious of their feelings, I try not to offend the hug-oriented section of our congregation, but that is sometimes difficult to do without throwing principle aside and allowing myself to become the subject of a warm, friendly embrace. Even our pastoral staff, six devout, mature, hard-working men of

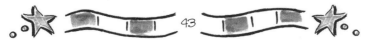

God, are divided between the hug and hug-not line.

Our senior pastor, Dennis Henderson, a former Dallas police officer, is not the hugging type. Craig Stonehocker (Children's Ministry and Adult Education), would rather undergo oral surgery than a squeeze from his fellow man. The four remaining leaders charged with the care of this particular flock are known huggers and therefore approached only while exercising extreme caution.

Prior to attending a major men's conference late last summer, I met with Pastor Craig to develop a polite, but—we hoped—effective policy directed at avoiding group grope sessions rumored to be common occurrences at these gatherings. Sharing a mutual concern for the feelings of the hug-oriented segment that might attend, we planned and strategized well into the wee hours until confident we had produced a foolproof line of defense.

We strategized until confident we had produced a foolproof line of defense.

"Let's go over it one more time," Craig said, "just to make sure we've got it right. I'll be sitting at the end of the row with you on my left—"

"Wait a minute," I said. "That leaves my left flank exposed to whoever happens to sit next to me. Why don't I sit at the end of the row, and you can sit on my left?"

"We've been over this," he said. "Why do you insist on harping over that point?"

"I know we've been over it, and I am not harping," I answered, "But I still don't see why I'm the guy taking all the risks here."

"Because I'm the pastor," Craig said. "Now tell me how you respond if a stranger approaches."

"I know this one," I said. "I reach out and offer my right hand to shake and firmly clasp his shoulder with my left, straight-arming him and keeping a respectable distance between us."

"Very good. Now you quiz me."

"OK," I said. "Here's a tough one. A guy walks up to you, obviously moved—let's say with tears in his eyes—and with outstretched arms reaches in your direction."

"Got it," Craig said. "I ball up my fist and hold it against my chest to maintain the MSD (Minimal Safe Distance). Am I right?"

"Perfect," I said. "It looks like we're as ready as we'll ever be, I guess."

The conference lasted two days and truly turned out to be a milestone event. Thousands of men from our area showed up to hear God's Word preached and to study its application. We heard speakers address nearly every issue that concerned us, from how to mentor our children to improving ourselves as husbands. What a weekend to share with sixty thousand men of God; I almost hoped it wouldn't end.

"That was some conference," Craig said as we made our way from the coliseum and back toward our car. "I'm glad we didn't miss it."

"Me too," I said. "I especially enjoyed the part about accountability and building our brothers in Christ."

"How about when the speaker called for all the clergy to come up front?" Craig asked. "There was such an overwhelming emotional response from the crowd that I actually shed a few tears."

"Yeah, me too," I said. And I could feel the tears returning. "You know what, Craig?" I asked.

"What?"

"You're not going to believe this," I said. "But I think I feel a hug coming on."

"Fight it, Darbee," he said, a hint of desperation in his voice. "Don't give in. You can whip this thing!"

"Oh come here, you crazy guy, you," I said and grabbed him around the upper torso.

His arms just flapped at his sides as I slapped him on the back in the middle of the coliseum parking lot. He didn't return my gesture, but you could tell how it moved him. He punched me in the arm before we reached the car.

Of Friends and Kids

Heavenly Sermons

In the middle of a long-winded sermon, a small child was overheard asking his mother: "Mommy, are you sure this is the only way we can get to heaven?"

—CAL AND ROSE SAMRA
FROM THE MOUTHS OF BABES

You Know There's a Baby in the House When...

Martha Bolton

- The only dinner music they're playing is "Barney's Greatest Hits."
- A bib is part of your place setting.
- They're serving teething biscuits instead of dinner rolls.
- The hostess offers you your beverage in a Sit 'n' Sip cup.
- All the eating utensils are rubber coated with Mickey Mouse handles.
- They're using Baby Wipes for napkins.
- The host offers to purée everyone's meat for them.
- The gravy has the distinct taste of formula.
- When the hostess offers you dessert, she spells it.
- The only accessories the hostess is wearing are a burp diaper on her left shoulder and a pacifier string around her neck.

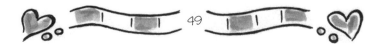

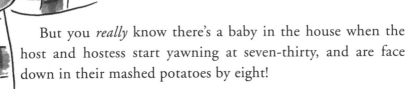

But you *really* know there's a baby in the house when the host and hostess start yawning at seven-thirty, and are face down in their mashed potatoes by eight!

Annual Letter

Lynn Bowen Walker

Save time! Keep up with friends without those bothersome phone calls or pesky in-person visits! Just five minutes filling in the blanks on our one-size-fits-all annual letter and you'll make each person in your address book feel as though you really care!

Dear_____,

What a _____(typical; superior; unsurpassed and really quite enviable) year it's been for our family! As we have been planning for some time, we finally took that trip to _____(the local petting zoo; the Grand Canyon; outer space). It was, of course, as spectacular as expected. Our family mastered the art of _____(making jewelry out of

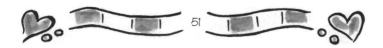

dried apple peels; synchronized spelunking; juggling flaming batons).

The kids spent the summer _____(playing All-County, All-League water polo; submitting videos of Dad repairing the roof to *America's Funniest Home Videos*; polishing up their matching Nobel prizes). We couldn't be prouder! Even the dog has learned to _____(heel; excuse herself before passing gas; program the VCR)! It has indeed been a wonderful year.

My husband is still busy at his job as _____(meat packer; disgruntled post office worker; King of Nova Scotia). It was a big year for him, as he finally got that _____(bunion operation; vasectomy; acquittal) we'd been waiting for.

Hope you and yours are all _____ (healthy; happy; chipping away at that high school degree). Give our best to _____(the old neighborhood; Larry the postman; rich old Uncle Edgar, who, as you know, we have always loved very, very much).

Our _____(sincerest wishes for a wonderful year; love and affection; cat just caught fire, so we have to go now),

_____

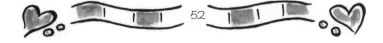

The Red Jell-O Caper
Barbara Johnson

One September evening, when my boys were young, I walked into the kitchen and found the two of them sitting at the kitchen table, scooping up red raspberry Jell-O in a spoon and then flinging it against the white brick wall at the end of the table. They were laughing and having such sport watching the red Jell-O drip down the white brick, making irregular tracks on the wall. Such fun—until I came in!

Imagine my shock and how stunned I felt! How should I react? What should I say? I could have dumped the remaining Jell-O on their heads and sent them packing. I could have screamed and hollered and laid a heavy discipline trip on them. It was up to me to act responsibly. Here I was, making memories for life. This was a moment they would always remember. Would I react or would I go bananas?

The shimmering bowl of red Jell-O was only half gone. Evidently very little had been eaten, but the bulk of it was thrown nicely against the white bricks. What a shame to waste the other half dish of Jell-O, when I could be in on the fun! They would have to clean it all up since they started it, but I would probably never have a better chance in my life to shoot Jell-O from the end of a spoon and watch it drip down the bricks, too!

So I sat down, put my purse on the floor beside me, picked up a *big tablespoon* (no sense fooling with teaspoons at this point), loaded up the spoon with a big glob of solid red stuff, and slung it carelessly against the wall. It was hilarious! I got another load on my spoon and let it fly. I could see why they had enjoyed this so much. Both of the boys decided I had made my decision to *enjoy* this, and they knew they would have to clean it all up, but now was time for fun.

So there we sat, all three of us, just slinging red Jell-O as fast as we could, and laughing until we almost cried. They were laughing part out of fear and part shame, too, but we used up all the Jell-O and the wall was just a wet, dripping, red mess. The white brick didn't have a spot where the Jell-O had missed trickling down.

Did I handle this wrong? I guess my sense of humor helped me decide it would be more fun to join in the fun than to jump up and down and scream. Besides, these are memories that are being built into kids. They will never forget that day. And neither will I. Maybe that is what is meant by "building laughter in the walls."

Even though this house is silent now, and the boys are gone, and there is no red Jell-O dripping down the wall, our laughter still echoes from the walls. My boys have laughter safe in their

own memories, too. Red Jell-O will *always* remind them of that day. I think my grandchildren will be told about the day that Barney threw all the Jell-O on the bricks (shooting it with a spoon), and how Grandma sat down and finished up the job with him.

Baby-U

Martha Bolton

The only parent who can truthfully say his child is perfect is God. Yet, from time to time, you'll run into one of "*them*"—those parents who are convinced their offspring have the I.Q. of Einstein, the looks of Tom Cruise, the athletic potential of Joe Montana, and the talent of the Three Tenors all rolled into one. Those parents have a knack for making you feel inferior if your child can't speak six languages by his first birthday and isn't on *Jeopardy* by the time he turns three.

I recall an encounter I once had. It took place in a park, and if my memory serves me correctly, it went something like this:

"What a cute baby," the woman commented as she parked her stroller next to mine.

"Thank you," I smiled. "Yours, too."

"Yes, he is, isn't he?" she beamed, releasing Junior to play.

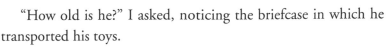

"How old is he?" I asked, noticing the briefcase in which he transported his toys.

"Eighteen months," she replied. "And yours?"

"He just had his second birthday last week."

"What's he taking?"

"Nothing," I shot back, slightly offended. "That toy is *his*."

"No," the lady said. "I mean, what *courses* is he taking? You know, to get ready for college."

"He's only two. He's not even in preschool yet."

"Are you saying your child isn't receiving any specialized training at all?" she gasped.

"Right now just 'potty.'"

"Think of the years you've wasted already."

"I haven't wasted any years," I insisted. "We play, we go for walks, I'm teaching him his alphabet."

"What about his SAT's?"

"They're part of the alphabet."

"Look, maybe it's not too late. Perhaps you could sign him up for some correspondence courses. You can teach him at home. Has he decided on his major yet?"

"He really hasn't said," I answered, playing along. "Maybe dentistry. He's been spending a lot of time with his teething ring lately."

"Dentistry? All the more reason that he should have a head start on his academics."

"I'll look into it," I smiled, in a discreet attempt to slide out of the conversation.

"But academics aren't everything," she continued, not letting me slide very far. "There are the arts, too. Have you exposed your son to the music of the great composers?"

"If you wind up his teddy bear, it plays 'Three Blind Mice.'"

"I assume it's safe to say you haven't started him on a musical instrument either."

"He's only two!" I protested. "Lifting a tuba now could give him a hernia."

"Look," she bragged, "our son is younger than yours and already he's quite skillful with the violin."

"I can see that. He's over there using it as a bucket in that sandbox."

"Junior!" she snapped, jumping to her feet. "Empty out that violin right now! You've got a recital in an hour!"

Junior proceeded to empty out the violin, she grabbed his hand, and marched off with him. "And then there's your swim lesson, your polo lesson, your dance class, your art instruction, your gymnastics class, your creative writing seminar . . ."

As their silhouettes began to fade into the distance, I paused long enough to wonder if maybe I *was* wasting time. Maybe we *should* fill every moment of our child's day with extracurricular activities and calculus tutors. But as I watched my son playing, as I heard his laughter, I decided instead to simply slow down and enjoy the day, the park—and my son's childhood—a little longer.

I Once Was Lost

G. Ron Darbee

"Spending some time alone with a group of boys may turn out to be the most satisfying experience of your life."

Thinking back on our youth pastor's words, I realize I may have been a little harsh when I referred to him as "that lying pagan." It's not as if he said "relaxing" or "pleasing" or "gratifying"; he said "satisfying." And I imagine that if you're twisted enough to become a youth pastor in the first place, you might be able to stretch your imagination to the point of calling the experience satisfying—satisfying in the same way that dislodging a fish hook from your index finger is satisfying, or removing your sneakers after running the Boston Marathon.

Greg's invitation to spend a weekend in the wilderness with ten fourth-grade boys was answered with something short of boundless elation on my part. Had it been just a simple invitation, I would have turned it down without a second thought. But

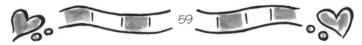

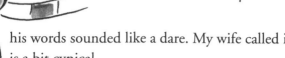

his words sounded like a dare. My wife called it goading, but she is a bit cynical.

"Come on, Ron, they're just kids!" Greg said, going for the soft underbelly of masculine pride. "What can they possibly do to you?"

"Will you listen to yourself?" I said. "Don't you remember Arlo Wilson? He wasn't always a tenor, you know!"

"He's not much of a tenor now," Greg said.

"That's not the point! They did that to him. They changed him."

"Well, Ron, if you're afraid—"

"Just hold on a minute," I said. "It's not like I'm scared or anything, it's just that—"

"No, Ron, really. I can ask Lewis," he said. "Maybe we can find an area of service that would better suit you. Say, the choir robes are looking a little worn. Do you sew, by chance?"

"Now, that's it," I demanded. "You're just going to have to find yourself another seamstress, Pastor. I'm going camping with those boys."

Sue stood at my side throughout the conversation, trying to remember where she stashed my backpack and sleeping bag. Call it women's intuition or just a mean streak, but she claimed to have known the outcome from the start.

"Pretty deft maneuvering, Einstein," she said, as we pulled away from the church. "By my estimation, you lasted all of two and a half minutes. A new record, I believe."

"Thank you, Dear. It's always nice to know I have your support."

Over the next two weeks, transportation arrangements were made, permission slips signed, and prayer networks established. My own prayer, offered up each morning, was simple and to the point. "Dear God, please watch over me as I venture into this

madness. Keep me safe and healthy, and help me to bring home a respectable percentage of the boys that I start out with."

D Day arrived, and, following the age-old tradition of rising at some ridiculously early hour before embarking on a journey, we departed. The bus ride to the mountains was uneventful, the boys passing time with a few ageless camp songs and a story or two. Sandwiches provided by the women's Bible study group were devoured en route, and I began to feel somewhat at ease. Maybe this wasn't going to be so bad after all.

Looking back with 20/20 hindsight, I realize it was at this point I should have been most concerned. Ten-year-old boys are notorious for their ability to lull you into a false sense of security. However, my mind somewhat dull for lack of sleep, I failed to recognize the warning signs. Our driver pulled into the staging area of Shadow Mountain Wilderness Refuge, and ten and a half smiles exited the bus.

> Looking back with 20/20 hindsight, it was at this point I should have been most concerned.

"Listen up," I instructed. "Grab your packs and sleeping bags, and form two lines by the trail, smallest boys in front. Yes, Alex?" I asked in response to a waving hand.

"How long will we have to walk?"

"About an hour," I replied. "From the looks of the map that Pastor Greg gave us, our campsite is about four miles in."

"Will there be Nintendo?" questioned another boy.

"No, no video games."

"Do they have cable?"

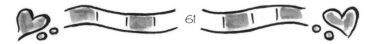

"No, there isn't any cable. There isn't even any 'they.' This is the wilderness!" I said, exasperated by the barrage of questions. "What is it, Matthew?" I growled at a youth, standing on tiptoe, waving his arms like a surrender flag.

"We used to have cable, but my dad didn't want it anymore."

"Enough with the cable already! Can we get on the trail before the Lord calls us home?"

"When is the Lord gonna call us home?" asked yet another boy.

"Soon, soon. Before I'm institutionalized, I'd like to think. Now get moving," I cried, and hurried the little mob toward the trail.

As we walked, I lost all track of time. Minutes seemed like hours as the tranquility of nature was interrupted by the complaints of the boys: "Emilio's stepping on the back of my shoes!"

I called the group to a stop, and we set down to ponder our situation.

"My feet hurt," and chorus after chorus of the ever popular "Are we there yet?" A glance at my watch gave me the first indication we might have strayed from our planned route.

"Does anyone remember coming to a fork in the trail?" I asked, trying to keep any hint of distress from my voice.

"I do," answered Alex.

"How far back was it?"

"I don't know."

"Wonderful. Your parents must be very proud. Does anyone else remember a fork?" weariness beginning to tell in my voice.

"I have a Power Ranger fork at home," volunteered Matthew.

"Let's head back this way for a while, and keep your eyes peeled for a fork in the path," I directed.

Two hours passed, and it was becoming noticeably quiet in the ranks. I called the group to a stop, and we set down to ponder our situation. Emilio and two others were perched on a fallen tree, giving fresh lyrics to old gospel tunes.

"I once was found, but now am lost—" sang the trio.

"Boys, I don't believe that is helping," I said. "Besides, I'm sure we'll find our way back to the right path soon. God won't let us wander around out here forever."

"God made the Israelites wander in the desert for forty years," whined Stewart. "You don't think we'll be here for forty years, do you?"

"No way," chided Emilio. "Mr. Ron would be dead by then."

"Emilio, much as I hate to disappoint you, there's a good chance that I may well be alive for another forty years, though I wouldn't give my mental faculties that many minutes. Anyway, I'm sure we'll all be just fine."

"Maybe we should pray or something," offered Alex.

"That's a good idea, Alex. Would you like to lead us?"

"OK. Dear heavenly Father, this is Alex. We love You and know You really love us back. Please take good care of us, and help Mr. Ron figure out where we are. Keep us safe, and don't let us get eaten by any bears or lions or stuff. And God, if we don't find the path real soon, please let Mr. Ron take us to McDonald's for dinner. Amen."

"That was just fine, Alex. Don't count on McDonald's though," I smiled, tousling his matted hair.

"Why not? We've been walking a long time, and I'm getting real hungry."

"Alex," I said, kneeling down to reason with the boy, "I know you're tired and hungry, but we're probably miles from the nearest fast-food restaurant."

"Nuh-uh," he replied, pointing past my shoulder. "There's one right over there."

"Over where?" I asked, dumbfounded.

"Through the trees," he responded, still pointing. "You can see the arches if you stand on that log."

Not sure if I should hug the child or just throw him for distance, I stood quietly for a moment, practicing some breathing techniques recalled from my days as a Lamaze coach.

"Alex," I asked, fighting to keep the smile on my face and my hands in my pockets. "Why didn't you tell me there was a McDonald's over there?"

"I didn't know you were looking for one. Is it near our campsite?"

A polite young man in a paper hat set us back on course, and we pitched camp for what turned out to be a wonderful—if somewhat less eventful—weekend. Bonds were formed and friendships strengthened. Boys learned the value of fellowship, and I may have learned a thing or two about a servant's heart.

The ride home was quiet, the troops a little subdued from the weekend's activities. We pulled into the church parking lot to the waves and shouts of parents and siblings. Pastor Greg clasped my shoulder as I collected my gear.

"Looks like things went pretty well."

"Not bad, really," I responded. "I feel kind of good about the whole thing."

"I knew you would," Greg replied. "Now next year—"

"Hold on," I said, backing into the side of the bus. "I don't think I'll be involved next year."

"Nonsense. Remember, 'He who began a good work in you will carry it on to completion.' I was just thinking, have you done any deep-sea fishing?"

A-flat

Chris Ewing

We don't entertain much. There is a very simple reason for this—
we just don't have very many repeat visitors. I'm not really sure
why this is, but I have my suspicions. One reason is that the
kitchen calendar is usually filled to the max with prior appoint-
ments and commitments. Another is that, like most homes with
younger children, our abode is not what you would particularly
call a very restful place—it is generally filled with more than its
share of sound, action, and peculiarities that make it a home.

We try to educate our children in the basics facts of etiquette—
really we do. Unfortunately, "Don't chew with your mouth open"
is a major topic of discussion around our dinner table. The
excuses for this nasty little mannerism are legion.

"But then I can't breathe!"

"That's why God made noses," I replied shortly.

"But mine is all clogged up," my daughter explained.

Oh. Then, by all means, go for it.

"Do you need to blow your nose?" my wife suggested.

My daughter nodded her head in agreement and grabbed her napkin.

"Not!" my wife and I echoed in unison. I slunk down in my chair as my wife continued the lesson.

"You leave the table to blow your nose, then wash your hands before returning."

My daughter got up to follow the suggestion.

"But leave your napkin here," I hastily added.

My brother and sister-in-law, who were dining with us, grinned at our futile training efforts. I shot an apologizing look at our guests as my son started to pound on his roll.

"Why are you doing that?" I asked.

"So I don't have to open my mouth so wide?"

Just then an outbreak of stifled coughing erupted from across the table.

"Please take smaller bites."

"Mmmmphh," replied my son.

"Say again?"

"Mmmm weary ungry."

"What? You're very hungry? But if you choke on that mouthful, you'll be very dead!" I said for the umpteenth time. "And don't talk with your mouth full. Okay?"

He looked at me with a confused look and bulging cheeks. He looked at his mother, to our honored guests, and back to me before spitting out his overloaded mouthful on his plate. I watched with amazement along with the other unbelieving folks at the table. When he was done, he said, "Okay," and started stuffing more food in.

My remaining child finished stirring her Jell-O into the mashed potatoes and gravy.

"Uh, I'm really not hungry anymore. I think I need to be excused, please. Like real soon."

That was understandable.

"What is this?" my son asked as he held up a cloth napkin.

"Oh," my brother-in-law answered for us. "That's to tie around your head so your hair doesn't get greasy from your hands."

"Cool!" my son said as he quickly tied the napkin around his head. The corner drooped down over one eye. "And how come we have a big fork and a little fork?"

"You'll be needing the other fork in just a few minutes," I explained. He gave me a quizzical look as he continued to stuff green beans into his mouth. Sure enough, not two minutes had gone by when one of his forks hit the floor.

He brightened up. "Oh, I see what you mean! Wow, you guys think of everything!"

When we were younger, we entertained more. Then the kids came along and we gradually gave up trying. I think the end of the road was after my son was born, for he was a very vocal child. He came out of the womb screaming and, well, never quite got over it.

My cousin was visiting us from out of state. It had been a long drive for her, but we were on her way home and she wanted to see the new addition to the family. I greeted her at the door and led her into the living room, where my small son lay sleeping on the floor.

"I'm sorry," she said as she glanced at the vacuum cleaner running in the corner. "I didn't mean to interrupt house cleaning."

"What was that?" I asked above the roar.

She pointed to the corner. "The vacuum. House cleaning. I'm sorry."

"I'm sorry, too," I said loudly. "I hate house cleaning."

My spouse joined us from the other room and we talked for a while as we stood over the sleeping babe. Finally, my cousin could stand it no longer.

"Uh, are you just going to leave the vacuum on?"

"Colic!" My wife shouted back. "We can't turn it off."

My poor relative looked at us like we had lost all semblance of sanity. "How can he sleep like that, with all that noise?"

"No, no, you don't understand," I tried to explain. "That's the only way he can sleep."

I led her over to the opposite corner of the room and pointed to several bare spots in the carpet.

My poor relative looked at us like we had lost all semblance of sanity

"This," I explained, "is where the vacuum ate the carpet threads before we realized we had to disconnect the brush." My daughter waved as she wandered through the room with stereo headphones on her head and trailing the cord behind her. Mufflers for the ears. She was no dummy.

"It's the colic," I repeated, as if that would explain everything.

My poor relative was getting a decidedly wild look in her eyes. I could tell she was seriously considering grabbing up the child and fleeing the house and the crazy people in it. I sighed and walked over to the noisy machine. I could hear that high A-flat pitch that meant the bearings were starting to go. I turned it off.

A deep, reverential silence settled over the house.

My cousin let out a shuddering sigh of relief.

My son woke up. He looked around. His face had that innocent, glowing look of a healthy newborn child, then it slowly contorted into a lopsided grimace.

"Uh oh," my wife said.

Another daughter wandered into the room with a friend. "There he is," said my daughter to her friend. "And he's gonna blow!" The children did an abrupt about-face and quickly fled the room.

"Maybe he's hungry," suggested my cousin.

"Just fed him."

"Maybe he's wet."

I checked. Dry as a summer in Wyoming.

The kid took a deep breath.

> I can still hit the exact pitch of the vacuum cleaner just before the bearings went.

"Waaaaaaaaaaa!"

It was starting again. I picked him up. I cooed, I rocked, I walked. His mother took over. She walked, she rocked, she cooed. Nothing would stop the high-pitched wail.

"Maybe," my cousin hollered, "you should take him to the doctor."

"The doctor is the one who suggested the vacuum. Besides, they won't let us come anymore," I explained. We had already tried that route and it had worked great for a while. We'd go to the doctor and the little guy would shut up as soon as we went through the door. Like a light switch. Got so we'd just hang out

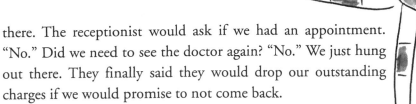

there. The receptionist would ask if we had an appointment. "No." Did we need to see the doctor again? "No." We just hung out there. They finally said they would drop our outstanding charges if we would promise to not come back.

I finally gave up, wandered back over to the cooled-down vacuum cleaner and turned it on. The pitch of the abused machine permeated the house, but within a minute the tortured child was asleep again.

My cousin began to get that wild look in her eyes again.

"My!" she shouted. "Look at the time! I have to make Omaha or Chicago or someplace before it gets dark."

"We were hoping you'd spend the night."

"Does he," she jabbed a finger in the direction of the Colic Kid, "sleep at night?"

"Depends on if the vacuum holds out or not," I explained.

Her eyes got real big. She left in a hurry. It was the last time I ever saw her. Last I heard, she still hadn't had any kids of her own.

Years later, I can still hit the exact pitch of the vacuum cleaner just before the bearings went.

It was, of course, an A-flat.

It makes a difference, of course, if you invite guests who have been, or are now at, the same point in life as you are currently. It provides for a common frame of reference.

"I've had to paint every room in the house," I explained to a recent guest, "about every other year—except this one." It was the laundry room, the one place you want to make sure everyone sees. I pointed out the grubby little finger marks and dented scuffs on the wall.

"See, here she was three, and these," I pointed out a black

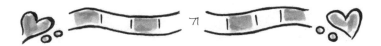

smear from a dirty little hand, "were from when she was four."

My friend nodded his head sagely. "My," he said, "she grew quite a bit that year!"

I beamed with pride.

"Yup."

"Hey," he said, "next time you're over, remind me to show you our family room. Got some good ones to show you."

I know we have entertained many angels in our home in our lives. Some of the faces were unfamiliar, some were sad when they came, some were happy, for one reason or the other, when they left. But it doesn't matter.

Some of those faces I know I will never see again in this life. Others, I wish I would see more often. But what really matters is that, at one time or another, they were there and that has made all the difference—if not in their lives, in ours.

Language Barriers
Martha Bolton

When my children were little, I used to get together with a group of other young mothers for a time of adult conversation. By "adult" I don't mean "x-rated." I mean engaging in discussions requiring words with more than one syllable.

Grown-ups spending too much time around toddlers can begin to lose their command of the English language. When this happens, take two dictionaries and call the doctor in the morning. At the supermarket I once overheard several young mothers who had evidently succumbed to "toddler tongue." Their conversation went something like this:

"Hey, you look terrific! But here . . . let me wipe off your chin . . . There, that's better."

"So, what have you been up to lately . . . (pinching cheek) besides growing up into a little lady?"

"*You* should talk. How old are you now?"

(Holding up fingers and flashing all ten of them three times.) "This many."

"My, my. You're getting to be such a BIG girl. Can you say 'bi-i-i-i-g girls?"

"I can dress myself."

"I can tie my shoes."

"I know all my multiplication tables."

"Do not."

"Do, too."

"Do not."

"*I'm an accountant! I do, too!* And what about you? Did you ever finish your doctorate?"

"Got my diploma last summer. It's hanging on the refrigerator."

There was a lull in the conversation as we all tried to remember the last time we had read a book that wasn't a pop-up, gone out to a restaurant that didn't have a clown maître d', or heard an eardrum-piercing high "C" note being hit by an entertainer instead of an eight-month-old.

We decided then and there that we all needed to get out more, to see the world, to expand our horizons . . . right after one more episode of *Sesame Street*.

Friends through It All

Old Friends

Old friends don't only know the real you, they prefer it.

—MARTHA BOLTON
DIDN'T MY SKIN USED TO FIT?

Friendship Is Blind

Charles Tindell

Roscoe and Wallace came out of the chapel one Sunday morning with arms locked, helping each other to use canes for balance. Their gait was unsteady but they were determined to help each other make it back to their rooms. It was heartwarming to watch and listen to these two joke and laugh about what they were doing. Wallace commented to his friend, "This is like the blind leading the blind."

What is so remarkable about Wallace's comment is that it was literally true. You see, both he and Roscoe are legally blind.

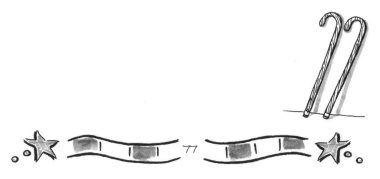

Girl Talk

Karen Scalf Linamen

I'm always trying to talk my friends into things.

Take this week for example. I've tried to talk a half dozen women into taking this class with me. It's an eight-week class and it's very reasonably priced and we'd be having fun and getting great exercise as well. What more could you ask for?

I just don't understand why I'm not getting any takers. I thought EVERYBODY harbored a secret wish to take belly-dancing lessons. I just don't get the reticence.

Maybe it's the Armenian blood in me. Either that or I spent too many hours as a kid watching *I Dream of Jeannie.*

No, wait, I bet I know what influenced me. No doubt it was that awesome photo of Liz Curtis Higgs in a veil and two pounds of eyeliner on the cover of her excellent book *Bad Girls of the Bible.* (There's no way you can convince me there's not a navel ring hiding beneath all those layers of silk!)

Be that as it may, so far my friends don't share my enthusiasm about the lessons. But I'll be sure to keep you informed.

The point is, my friends and I are always swapping ideas on how to make our lives more interesting or productive or healthy. Okay, so I'll admit the belly-dancing brainstorm might have been a little over the top. Normally our ideas are much more mainstream.

Like the way we're always swapping diet strategies and news-flashes. Last week, for example, I got a phone call from a friend of mine. She sounded positively manic as she squealed, "You'll never guess what happened last night!"

I wondered if she had won the lottery. I was getting ready to ask her to pay for my belly-dancing lessons when she said, "I got into my blue jeans!"

She hasn't worn blue jeans in a year. But after dieting and exercising for several weeks, she got those denims zipped.

I understand the significance of her news. I've fought the battle of the bulge myself. The truth is, winning the lottery pales in comparison to getting back into a favorite pair of jeans after a cellulite-induced exile.

We also encourage each other when it comes to beauty secrets.

And, boy, do we need those beauty secrets. Can anyone explain to me why, as we get older, our eyebrows, lips, hair, and bones get thinner while our waistlines continue to thicken? It hardly seems fair.

Not to mention what happens to our eyelids. Last week my friend Beth lamented, "It's getting harder to put on eyeliner. My eyelids are too wrinkly."

I know what she's talking about. It's not easy getting liner up and down both sides of all those tiny wrinkles.

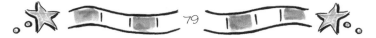

Half the time my eyelids sport a dotted line.

I have good news on the hair removal front, though. I had an appointment for electrolysis to remove a dozen stubborn chin hairs. I've had more than one reader write and ask me how it went. Here's the report: I love the results! You'll be glad to know that my chin stubble days are behind me. I no longer look like Michael W. Smith, which is thrilling to me although my fourteen-year-old daughter says she misses snickering at my rendition of "Rocketown."

Electrolysis tip: take a Walkman and listen to your favorite music as your hair follicles are getting zapped. And turn the beat up loud—with enough decibels it's possible to drown out some of the pain. (But not too loud. Your electrologist will be determining the voltage via a foot pedal. You do NOT want her tapping her toes to the beat. Trust me on this.)

And when my friends and I aren't trading health and beauty secrets, we can often be found talking about the relationships in our lives. We ask each other questions like these . . .

How can I teach my kids to be more respectful? How can I forgive my husband? How can I encourage a friend who's going through a tough time? I'm lonely—how can I create more meaningful bonds with the people around me? How can I get rid of the anger I feel toward my ex? How can I get my kids to be more responsible? Do I criticize my husband too much? If so, how can I build him up instead? How can I set boundaries at work? How can I get along better with my parents?

From there the categories get even broader. The Bible says God forgives me for my past mistakes—why can't I seem to forgive myself? How can I stay consistent in God's Word? Why do I have a hard time believing Jesus loves me? How can I experience

more power in my prayer life? I'm struggling with lust or envy or bitterness—any suggestions how I can win this battle? How can I get a handle on my depression? I can't seem to trust God about my situation—how can I learn to trust him more?

I love having these kinds of conversations with my friends. And if you're not broaching these kinds of topics with godly girl-friends in your life, maybe you should give it a try.

I find that my friends are a wealth of practical information. No one friend has all the answers, but between them all I've gathered useful insights on everything from fixing my cat to fixing my marriage, from bleaching my teeth to harnessing my tongue, from balancing my checkbook to balancing my life.

And what's really great is that you and I can have these kinds of intimate, encouraging conversations with our friends anytime, anywhere. We don't have to make a formal appointment! We can encourage each other over coffee at our kitchen tables, via cell phones as we commute home from work, or side by side as we browse garage sales or watch our kids play softball.

In fact, I was sort of hoping Thursday nights would provide an opportunity for these kinds of conversations with my friends as we drove to our belly-dancing classes.

If that sounds like fun to you, give me a call.

As of this moment, there's still plenty of room in the car.

With Nuts or Without?

Laura Jensen Walker

I met my best friend Lana when she visited a home Bible study I attended. When she first walked in the door in her short red dress, blonde "tilted" hairstyle (she had one of those asymmetrical cuts that were popular in the late '80s), and long red fingernails, I thought, *This girl needs Jesus!*

Right then and there, I made it my mission to show her "the way."

After the study, I promptly cornered her in the living room where she was enjoying a bowl of ice cream, backed her up against the wall, and shared my colorful testimony with her. I wouldn't say that I bowled her over, but I definitely made an impression. I was wearing slipper socks with baggy gray sweats that bore the faint signs of a recent accident with a chocolate ice-cream cone, and my unpolished nails were ragged from that

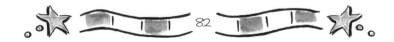

afternoon's biting session. (I was living with my friends Pat and Ken at the time—hosts of the home Bible study.)

Well, Lana already *had* Jesus—she'd become a Christian just a few weeks earlier—but she was still finding her way in this whole new world of Christianity. And I could tell that she needed my help in the dressing-for-the-Lord department.

Keeping in mind that she was a "baby" Christian and didn't know any better, I diplomatically suggested that maybe Jezebel-red wasn't the *best* color to wear to a Bible study.

Perhaps a nice demure floral print instead—that maybe covered her knees? And while she was at it, she might want to trim those flashy fingernails just a teensy-weensy bit, and consider going a little easier on the makeup?

This from a woman whose eyelashes hadn't seen mascara in over a month.

Thankfully, Lana didn't hold my well-meaning but INSANE suggestions against me, and she recognized the broken heart beneath the bravado.

I told her that I too once dressed in power suits and silk Dynasty-style dresses with mega–shoulder pads until I saw the light. Then I sold my collection for pennies to the dollar in favor of the standard good Christian woman's "uniform": subdued colors, demure floral dresses with lace collars—always calf- or ankle-length—and low-heeled pumps or sandals.

My former fiancé had taught me the proper Christian woman uniform code and pointed out a couple women in the congregation whose godly dressing examples he thought I should follow. He'd also taught me that since a woman's crowning glory was her hair, long hair was really more spiritual.

However, after we broke up, I began to rebel.

I chopped off all my hair (which I'd grown out in an effort to please him) in a moment of anger.

My sweet young niece ran into the same problem with a guy she once dated. (Amazing the things we'll do when we're head over heels, or infatuated.) Her ex-boyfriend also insisted that she have long hair, wouldn't allow her to wear a second modest earring in her ear, and nixed the idea of colored nail polish, other than red at Christmastime.

After their breakup, she started to become friends with a nice guy at church and, like many single women longing to be married, wondered at first if perhaps there *might* be the possibility of a romantic future. That possibility was abruptly squelched when he came up to her and said, "Don't you think your lipstick's a little too bright for church?"

Lana and I looked at each other and knew that this was the place God wanted us.

My new friend Lana, "baby" Christian that she was, knew better than either me or my niece who had grown up in the church, that outward appearance didn't make the woman.

That's why they call it "freedom" in Christ.

So she encouraged me to go with her to a Friday night singles group at a large, popular, cutting-edge church in town that we'd both heard about. And neither of us was ever the same again.

Talk about freedom.

When we first walked in, we saw men with earrings (in one or both ears), a few with blue or purple Mohawks, shaved heads

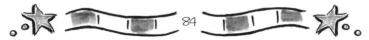

(most of them men), and women in leather pants or short skirts and sporting multiple safety-pin earrings. We also saw lots of jeans and T-shirts, and even a couple conservative blouses and floral print skirts. As long as certain body parts weren't exposed, the dress "code" was pretty much "anything goes."

And the music was great. One very cute guy and a guitar.

But the best part of all came when the newly married singles pastor began to teach. He spoke to us about love and acceptance and the difficulties that we as singles faced: the longing to be married, the struggle to stay pure, the sense of isolation, the need for friendship . . . and the freedom in Christ.

Lana and I looked at each other and knew that this was the place God wanted us.

After a year of faithful attendance, we were both invited to join the singles leadership group, where we headed up the social events. And boy, did we ever have the social events! Game nights, movie nights, picnics, scavenger hunts, theme potlucks, and even a huge Hawaiian luau at our house one summer.

By this time, Lana and I had moved into a two-story Mediterranean style four-bedroom house with two other single girls from church. It was a huge house, complete with swimming pool, hot tub, and a large backyard just perfect for parties. But the décor left a lot to be desired: sixties shag carpet in every hue of the rainbow—the living room was royal-blue-and-green blend, the family room, orange-and-black, the master bath, fire-engine red, Lana's bedroom, lime green, and mine, screaming hot pink.

The tacky carpet didn't inhibit our party appetite though.

We'd have old movie nights and watch *Casablanca, The African Queen,* or our favorite musicals like *West Side Story.* Only problem was, a couple of the guys in our group kept blocking our

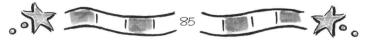

view as they jumped up and tried to pirouette and *grande jete* in concert with the Sharks and the Jets on-screen.

We almost lost the TV to a twirling twosome gone awry.

And the luau with more than a hundred people is still being talked about.

We wanted to roast a whole pig in a pit in the backyard but we thought we might not get our rental deposit back if we dug too deep, so we settled for kahlua pork instead, slow-cooked overnight in the oven. We had a pineapple-eating contest and a hula hoop contest, and I smashed a cream pie—one in each hand—into the faces of two of the guys (which landed me sopping wet in the pool).

Or wait, did that happen at the guys' birthday party? Can't remember. Too many parties, too little memory now.

Then there was the birthday party we'll never forget.

Lana was about to turn twenty-eight, and I asked her how she wanted to celebrate the occasion. Did she want a huge potluck bash? Perhaps pizza and a movie? An ice-cream social?

None of the above.

She'd had her fill of potlucks and pizza and the same-old, same-old, and wanted something completely different for her special day. So we decided to host a formal, intimate "black-tie" dinner. Actually, it wasn't necessary that the guys wear tuxes, but some kind of tie was mandatory.

No tie, no dinner.

When Lana handed me the guest list, it consisted of six men and just one other girlfriend (who came late, so for a while our odds were three-to-one). She'd chosen the guy she was interested in at the time, as well as the one I was interested in, even though neither had yet to return the interest. We kind of considered

them our first string. Next came the second string: the two guys who were our backups in case things didn't work out with Bachelor Number Ones. And finally, the benchwarmers—on the off chance that neither Bachelor Number Ones nor Twos fell head over heels for us.

In the mood to play dress up, Lana and I both wore smart black cocktail dresses a la Doris Day, sparkly rhinestone earrings, and black stockings with the seams that go up the back. What can I say? We grew up on Doris and Cary and were in a fifties frame of mind.

Remembering our "no tie, no dinner" rule, the men did themselves proud. Every single one was sporting a tie or something vaguely resembling one around his neck. Okay, so one guy would've taken

One guy would've taken first place in the ugly tie contest with his shrieking orange-plaid polyester.

first place in the ugly tie contest with his shrieking orange-plaid polyester, and another was wearing a clip-on, but we didn't want to press our luck.

We were just glad that all the guys showed up.

The menu for the evening was beef stroganoff and Caesar salad (long before the days of salad-in-a-bag, so it was all from scratch). And for dessert, cherries jubilee.

Ooh la la.

Since we only had stoneware place settings for four, we borrowed my mom's fine china, silver, and stemware. She even graciously loaned us her best linen tablecloth and napkins. The candlelit table was gorgeous and gleaming, the food delicious, and the repartee sparkling. It was a perfect evening.

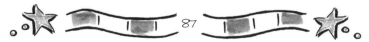

Then it happened.

Benchwarmer number one—who resisted anything formal—loudly blew his nose in my mom's linen napkin. (If you're hearing this for the first time, Mom, don't worry; we had it dry-cleaned.)

Scratch that one from the lineup.

Actually, we never married any of those guys. Instead, God brought us the "ringer" first stringers he'd picked out for us long ago. Okay, I know I'm mixing my sports metaphors here, but they both have to do with a ball, so it works for me.

Lana and I have fun no matter what we do.

I'll never forget years ago when we went to see the movie *Ishtar* with Warren Beatty and Dustin Hoffman. We thought it was a scream and laughed our heads off in the theater.

We were the only ones. No one else even chuckled.

The film was one of the biggest bombs in movie history. When we watched it again a few months later on video, we looked at each other over bowls of chocolate ice cream—hers had nuts, mine didn't—and shrieked, "What *were* we thinking?"

Make a Friend...Again

Karen Scalf Linamen

It all started when my sister Michelle blurted, "Let's call Brenda. Right now. Don't even think about it! Let's just do it."

We were in Michelle's home office. She was sitting by her computer. I was across the desk from her, painting my nails. I looked up, "Really? Now? After seven years?"

We had once been really close, the three of us. The silly nicknames and private jokes we shared could have filled volumes. We grew up together, really, and at one time the good memories had run as freely as milk and honey.

Then seven years ago something happened. Not a fight, really, just a concentrated time of stress and transition, and before we could smooth everything out, Brenda's divorce swept her down her own private path of emotional crisis, and my struggles with clinical depression swept me in an entirely different direction. As for Michelle, she had her hands full as she married, separated for

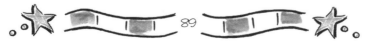

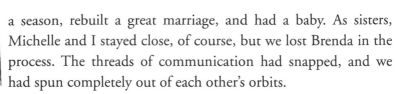

a season, rebuilt a great marriage, and had a baby. As sisters, Michelle and I stayed close, of course, but we lost Brenda in the process. The threads of communication had snapped, and we had spun completely out of each other's orbits.

Michelle didn't blink an eye, "Yeah. Right now. After seven years. I'll dial."

I held the cordless extension gingerly with wet fingernails and watched Michelle dial the other phone.

Ring.

Ring.

Ring.

"Hello?"

Michelle said, "Hi, Brenda, this is a voice from your past."

I said, "Two voices."

Brenda said, "I have no idea who you are. Who is this?"

Michelle said, "You have to guess. We wanted to say hi. We miss you."

Brenda said, "You DO sound sorta familiar . . ."

I said, "I see we're going to have to sing."

Michelle said, "Sing?"

I said, "Yes, sing. You know the song. Ready? One, two, three . . ."

So we sang "Burn, Cookie, Burn." You can stop trying to recall the tune from some national countdown. The only time and place it has ever been performed is around midnight in the orange and gold kitchen in my parents' house on Farm Street back in the mid-'70s. You see, Brenda, Michelle, and I were baking cookies when we began pretending the cookies were talking to us from the oven and—

No. We weren't on drugs. We were teenagers and punchy with life and with the lateness of the hour, and it really did seem pretty

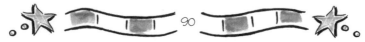

hysterical at the time, and I'm not even going to TRY to explain it for one more second. You just have to believe me. It was funny at the time.

And somehow, it was funny again last week, when Brenda's voice suddenly broke into laughter and we heard her squeal, "You GUYS, what ARE you doing?" and the tentative tendrils of reconnection touched and caught and held, and suddenly we were kids again and friends.

It was a very good moment.

And I have Michelle to thank for it.

It takes courage to reach out across a rift. Michelle was brave. And wise. More so than I. I just got to tag along and reap the benefits.

We met the next day for lunch. Brenda saw photos of Michelle's baby and met my five-year-old for the first time. Her son, Blake, had been six months old when I'd seen him last—now there are hockey trophies on his bedroom walls.

I think we'll hang on better this time. I also think we are lucky. I think second chances are too special to squander.

Sistership
Patsy Clairmont

Friendship is the ship the Lord often launches to keep my boat afloat. I seem to require people in my life. Scads of them. I am not the type who wants to be an island unto myself. (Unless it's Gilligan's Island.) Not that I don't want to be alone; my alone times are precious to me. I guard them and find solitude necessary for my sanity (well, what's left of it). Yet interacting with others encourages, nurtures, challenges, hones, and helps refine me. My journey has been made more joyous by connecting with friends.

One of my favorite dots in my network of friends is Carol. We are friends with history. We go back to the days when gumdrops were the latest rage in shoes. (Anyone remember those? They were a jazzed up version of saddle shoes.)

Carol and I still tell each other secrets and giggle over our silly flaws. We know the worst about each other and choose to believe

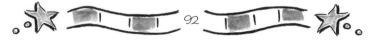

the best. We have not always known how to do that. Then Jesus entered our lives and our friendship. He taught us important skills in esteeming one another. In our thirty-nine years of relationship, we have never not been friends; but since we met the Lord, our friendship has deepened in appreciation and affection.

We love to shop, decorate, antique, travel, dream, and scheme with each other. We have gone through the best of times in our families and the worst of times. We have celebrated and sorrowed together. We have guffawed and groaned. We have worshiped the Lord at the same church and studied the Scriptures in our homes. We have at times let the other one down, which gave us an opportunity to learn the imperative friendship skill of forgiveness.

Even though we share many interests, we are opposite personalities. I am boisterous; Carol is reticent. I'm a right-now person; she's an I-can-wait gal. Even physically we are opposites. She towers over my pudgy frame. Her hair is wispy and straight while mine is bushy and frizzy. Differences and similarities along with years of caring and sharing have enhanced our sistership.

Just three weeks ago I moved. I moved only seven blocks, but I still had to pick up everything and find a place to set it down in my new abode—that or have an enormous (thirty-four years' worth of stuff) yard sale. Thankfully, I had dear friends come to my rescue and help me pack.

After arriving in our new home, I was overwhelmed with the prospect of settling in. I had thought I would pull it together rapidly. Instead, I roamed from room to room trying to remember my name. Carol came to give support (and to verify my identity) every morning for four days. She assisted me until early evening, when she would then make our dinner, serve us, and clean up.

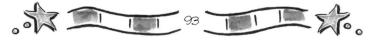

You can only guess what a gift that was to me emotionally. I never expected that kind of beyond-the-call-of-duty effort, but I'm certain our new home ownership would have found me sinking before I could even unload the cargo, if it were not for Carol's life preserver of kindness.

What is it about moving that is so disassembling? The leaving of the old? The adjusting to the new? The disheveling of all our stuff? The initial sense of unconnectedness? Or all of the above? Carol's and my long-term connectedness served as a stabilizer during this turbulent time. And it was great to have someone with similar tastes to bounce ideas off of about furniture placement, window treatments, and picture arrangements.

By evening, when my wagon was draggin', Carol could catch her second wind and perform wonders in the kitchen. This girl can cook! Every night her feast renewed our strength and our determination to get back at it. The following day we would eat the leftovers for lunch, and in the evening she would prepare yet another culinary delight.

I'm thankful that the Lord knew we would need each other to survive various storms—and that he made available the harbor of friendship.

With Friends Like These

Luci Swindoll

One of the most delightful weekends I had spent since moving to California six months before was nearing an end. Two teenage girls approached me while I was counting out my vitamins. "What are all those pills for?" one of them asked. "Well," I explained, "these two are for beautiful eyes, this one is for long willowy legs, that little one is for pearly, white teeth . . ." and as I was waxing on, the other girl interrupted me with, "Haven't been taking them long, have you?"

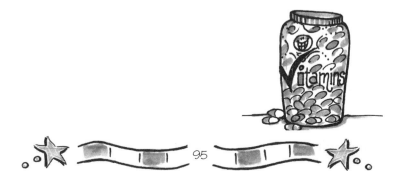

Don't Look at Me

Tim Wildmon

One August afternoon I was in our front yard pitching the baseball to my then four-year-old son Wesley while he tried to hit it with his bat. He loves for me to play ball, any kind of ball, with him. I would toss the ball from ten feet or so and he would swing just as hard as he could, but this time, again and again, he was missing the ball. After fifteen minutes or so, I looked at Wesley—knowing that he had hit the ball well the last time we played and that he had a genetic advantage over your average four-year-old—and asked, "What's the problem? Why can't you hit the ball?"

Immediately, and with a "how dare you ask me that" tone in his voice, Wesley replied: "You not (that's right, *you not*) throwin' ball where bat is."

"What?" I said as I processed his words. *You know, that's not a bad comeback from a four-year-old who doesn't use verbs*, I thought.

I really didn't know how to respond. In all my years in baseball, I had never heard that one before.

I can just see this excuse catching on in the Big Leagues. I can just hear a Cardinals slugger going back to the dugout after being struck out by Greg Maddox: "You saw it, coach. I put the bat right over the plate and Maddox completely missed it. I don't know why you're looking at me; your problem is right out there on the mound."

Why is it that we human beings have such a difficult time taking responsibility for our own actions? Why do we have such a hard time accepting blame when we do something wrong or when something we attempt fails? Passing the buck is as old as the Garden of Eden.

One of my worst memories from my five years at Pierce Street Elementary School in Tupelo, Mississippi, was the day I decided to rebel against authority—The Man, if you will—who was always trying to keep us kids down. The Man was Mr. Harry Armstrong, the principal. One of the ways The Man (who, in retrospect, was a really nice guy only doing his job) oppressed us kids was to not allow us near the Purrell's Pride chicken truck when it came around once a week to deliver food—namely chickens—to our cafeteria.

"Let me remind you, students, to stay away from the chicken truck during recess," Mr. Armstrong would say over the intercom. He said this often. "This could be dangerous and someone could get hurt."

One day during recess three other third-grade rebels—Greg, Jim, Eddie—and I decided to unshackle the chains of repression and take a step on the Wild Side. The refrigerated chicken truck had arrived—which was about the size of a large U-Haul—and

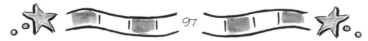

the driver had opened the doors to the back and gone inside the cafeteria.

"Well, there it is," Jim said. "Well, are we or aren't we?"

"Let's go," said Greg.

"Yeah, let's go over there and see what's inside," said Eddie.

I remained silent but decided I too would see what lurked in the back of the forbidden chicken truck. So we snuck over from the playground to the back of the truck and looked in. Lo and behold, what should we find but a truck full of frozen chickens! In the back of a chicken truck! Imagine that!

"So, this is what the inside of a chicken truck looks like, it's slap full of frozen fowl?" I said.

"Fowl?" said Jim. "I don't smell anything." I was always the one with the advanced vocabulary. That's why I'm a writer and the others are making a lot of money with jobs that don't require complete sentences. This is how my friends make a living now:

"You need?"

"Not sure."

"Oh, you need!"

"How much?"

"Not much."

"Come down?"

"A little."

"Okay."

"Sold!"

Or something like that.

Well, as fate would have it (or predestination for you Presbyterians), the cafeteria manager and truck driver came out and caught us dead-to-rights. (What does this term mean? I have

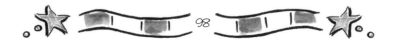

no idea, but I've heard it all my life.) Yes sir, we were in the very act of standing around looking dumb in the back of the Chicken Truck.

I just stood there dumbstruck. There's nothing you can do or say at this point. I mean, we're in the back of the strictly-off-limits chicken truck while our classmates are on the playground and the mean old cafeteria lady is staring right at me. I couldn't run. I couldn't, like, say, "Oh, look over there, Johnny Wilson's throwin' dirt clods at little Miss Lane again," and then jump out of the truck. The oldest trick in the book, that of distraction, wouldn't work at this point. No way. I didn't even think about it anyway. I just stood there waiting for her to do or say something bad.

"Children, to the office now!" said the mean old cafeteria manager, a lady whose name I've long since forgotten. My heart started to pound at the thought of what our punishment might be. Forget "our," I was worried about *my* hide. What to do? What to say? Who could be

My daddy was a preacher. I couldn't be responsible for turning these kids into juvenile delinquents.

the fall guy for us? Surely Greg, Jim, or Eddie would be a man and take the blame so all of us wouldn't have to get a whoopin'. John Wayne would. I would have, but my daddy was a preacher. My daddy was "Brother Don," pastor of Lee Acres United Methodist Church just a mile from the school. I couldn't be responsible for turning these other three kids, whose dads had pagan jobs, into juvenile delinquents and have this put on my Permanent Record and disgrace my dad and our family! This

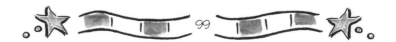

would kill my sweet momma. Just kill her.

I tried begging, pleading, and everything else to avoid going to see Mr. Armstrong. "Did I ever tell you you make the best fried chicken in the South?" I lied, looking up at the mean old cafeteria manager as she escorted us down the long, long hallway to The Office. "Forget the South, how 'bout the world? Really, I've eaten a lot of fried chicken in my day and I'm tellin' you, yours is absolutely the finest. Colonel Sanders couldn't lick your lard, ma'am."

We had been caught dead-to-rights, which obviously was a very, very bad way to get caught.

My false flattery didn't work. There we stood in the office before The Man himself.

"Mr. Armstrong, these young men were up in the back of the chicken truck, I caught 'em dead-to-rights," said the mean old cafeteria manager lady.

"Did, huh?" said Mr. Armstrong sternly, looking at the four of us in a single-file line. I was the tallest—or at least felt that way—and my neck was sticking out like a "hey-look-at-me-I-did-it" giraffe. "Caught 'em dead-to-rights, did you?"

"Yes sir, dead-to-rights."

"Well, boys, we've been over this rule a thousand times, haven't we now?"

I began to look away and scratch my head as I pondered the honesty of this statement. A hundred maybe, but a thousand? Should I challenge this, prove The Man wrong, see if he wouldn't back down a little while scoring a few points with the boys in the process?

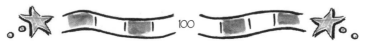

"Mr. Wildmon, look at me when I talk to you, son."

Nope. Bad idea.

"Yes sir."

"Well, boys, you weren't just caught now, were you? You were caught dead-to-rights."

This sounded worse than just your basic case of getting caught, I thought. We had been caught dead-to-rights, which obviously was a very, very bad way to get caught. I began to wonder, *Why hadn't my parents ever told my about this dead-to-rights thing? Why was The Man using the word "dead" so much here? Did he have the authority to carry out capital punishment?*

Well, we each confessed to the obvious, repented, and received one swift, not-so-friendly reminder to stay away from the chicken truck before we returned to the friendly confines of the playground. But the important lesson I learned that day was I needed to be quicker on my feet with creative excuses when caught doing something terribly wrong like climbing up in the chicken truck. So that about wraps up this story and . . .

What? Excuse-making and blaming is the American way, no? Actually, the very valuable lesson made clear to me that day was that there were consequences to my actions and when I had done wrong, it was better just to confess, come clean, and not try and make excuses—often dishonest excuses—for my wrongdoing.

Well, I guess Wesley will learn more clearly how to accept responsibility in a couple of years when he swings and misses three times in a real game, and the umpire yells, "Strike three, you're out!" and sends him back to the dugout. In the meantime, dear old Dad will work on him as the Lord God works on me.

Now, when to tell him about dear old Dad and the chicken truck escapade? It wasn't actually my fault, you know. I just kind

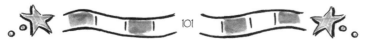

of got mixed up with the wrong crowd and, well, one thing led to another and then there was this giant frozen chicken that came to life. Yeah, that's it! Now, I'm not talkin' your average giant frozen chicken, oh no. No, no. I'm talkin' a Big Bad Boneless Giant Frozen Chicken that could whoop Godzilla without any problem and would terrorize the other children if not for me and my buddies . . .

5

Real Men Do Have Friends

Golf Buddies

My friend Gord and I have an agreement:
If he beats me at golf, I buy him lunch. If I
beat him, he accuses me of cheating.

—PHIL CALLAWAY
WHO PUT MY LIFE ON FAST-FORWARD?

Craziness Loves Company
Phil Callaway

When I was just a boy my mother told me, "Son, choose your friends as you would your books. Few, but good." I was six months old at the time, so I didn't have a clue what she meant. But as I got older I began to get the point. Just as life's joys are multiplied when shared with a friend, so the weight of life's burdens can be cut in half. One of those few but good friends in my life is Gord Robideau. He's crazier than a loon, and he needs a lot of help, so we have some things in common. When Gord brought home a collie puppy and named it Sabre, he hung up this sign:

WARNING! GUARD DOG!
SURVIVORS WILL BE PROSECUTED!

A nicer guy you're unlikely to find. A better looking, wealthier guy, perhaps. But not a nicer one. Gord is one of those rare people who asks you how you're doing, then sticks around for the answer.

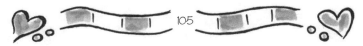

He puts his fingers on my faults without rubbing it in. Our friendship was forged around backyard barbeques and late night walks when I would pour out the contents of my troubled heart. Gord listened. I don't remember great words of wisdom, though there may have been some. I just remember that he walked with me.

Geezer Guys

Dave Meurer

This is the poignant tale of two dads, two lifelong friends, two con-
versations, and the passing of two decades. Sadly, the writer is not
fabricating any of this.

Years ago my roommate Tim and I used to sit around our
apartment late at night discussing the nature of man, or eschatology,
or some heavy spiritual tome by Charles Spurgeon, or even the
seventh chapter of Romans. We would say things like this:

TIM: So, do you think the man Paul is describing in Romans
7 is himself as an unbeliever, as a believer, or just a theoretical
man cast in the first person as a rhetorical device?

ME: Um, not a rhetorical device. I think it is definitely personal, but I don't know how you can square the despairing language with the triumphant tone of Romans 8. It has to be past
tense.

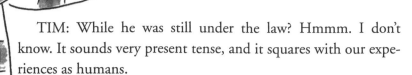

TIM: While he was still under the law? Hmmm. I don't know. It sounds very present tense, and it squares with our experiences as humans.

ME: But since when do we measure objective truth by our personal experience?

This would go on for *hours*.

Fast forward to a recent call from Tim, and note how our conversation reveals the subtle nuances of our maturing process:

TIM: Hey, my kid gave me one of those nose-hair trimmers for my birthday!

ME: An entire appliance just to trim your nose hairs? How pathetic. Why don't you just use the sideburn trimmer that comes with your razor? That's what I do.

TIM: But then you have to hold it upside down and at weird angles. This is much more efficient.

ME: Tim, listen to us. We are talking like geezers. We used to talk about big things, important things, *deep* things—and now we're talking about the best way to remove excess hair from our nostrils.

Pause.

TIM: Well, it works for ear hairs too.

ME: Really? I hate ear hairs. How much did it cost?

"We used to talk about big things, important things, deep things."

While a surface comparison of those two conversations may make it seem that Tim and I have been transformed from keenly spiritual young men into profoundly oafish old coots, you really have to hear the rest of the conversa-

tion before you can confirm that you are correct.

Wait a minute. That didn't sound right. What I mean to say is that you need to keep listening before you come to any conclusions.

Continuing on . . .

TIM: You know, as I get older I can understand the panic that middle-aged guys feel. It's the mid-life crisis. We are all getting older, we are sprouting nose and ear hairs, and we can actually see our youth slipping away from us. If I didn't have heaven to look forward to, I would probably panic too.

ME: Yeah. The big yellow bulldozer of time is shoving us to the edge of eternity and there are no brakes. It all happened so fast. Life is a vapor. I don't know what I would do if I didn't have a future to look forward to beyond the here and now. Ultimately, we end up in the presence of God. That keeps me focused. It gives me hope.

TIM: Plus, I'm in better shape than you. Do you ever actually exercise? Other than pumping forks?

ME: Listen, bifocal eyes, at least I'm not wearing the glasses my grandfather wore.

TIM: Putz.

ME: Dork.

TIM: Dweeb.

ME: Geek.

We then hang up.

Tim and I were in the third grade together. We went through high school together. We were in each other's wedding. Our toddlers played together in a big cardboard box in Tim and Pam's living room—a box we eventually packed with stuff as we helped them move away.

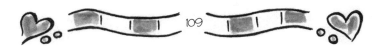

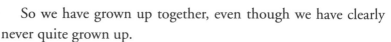

So we have grown up together, even though we have clearly never quite grown up.

Our wives are amazed at just how rapidly we revert to our junior high school mentalities when we get together—even tossing friendly insults we pull from the dusty attic of our memories.

"Just listen to them," Pam will say, shaking her head.

"I really don't know what gets into them," Dale has replied on more than one occasion.

What gets into us is simply our boyhood.

We look like men. We are husbands and fathers, and ostensibly even professionals. Tim is a college professor, for cryin' out loud. His students would be shocked.

But deep down, there is a part of us that desperately wants to hold on to the days of our youth. The crazy, more carefree days of hanging out with our friends. That's why we sometimes act like, well, our kids.

That can be an innocent enough impulse, and even positive. It can be energizing. In a sort of reliving the past—in a short visit or brief phone call to a childhood friend—we take a small vacation from the pressures of today. Innocent immaturity can be a blast for a while.

The danger is when a desire to revisit the past turns into raw panic over all the roads not traveled. Despair over the missed opportunities. The burning desire to know what could have been, even though logic tells us it cannot now be.

I think all guys are gripped with those feelings sometimes. And that is when we have to wrench ourselves back to the present and somehow get a grip. We may even need to call that old friend and admit, "This is what I'm feeling like. Talk sense into me!"

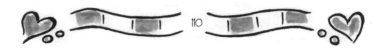

Too many dads about my age do really stupid stuff when they panic. And they hurt their families.

Oh, and about the identity of the man in the seventh chapter of Romans? The guy who felt wrenched because he was sorely tempted to do the very things he hated, and felt often unable to do the things he knew were right? I finally figured out who he is.

He's me. And he's you. We're all in this together.

So, dads, listen up for a minute. Get really close, and listen carefully. Pretend I am a very old friend giving you some heartfelt advice.

You are a dad now. You are not a little boy, nor are you a teenager. You can still play and have fun, but you are never going back to your youth. All the roads before you lead in one direction— toward tomorrow, not yesterday. Take a deep breath. Realize that you are moving slowly, but surely, toward the God who made you. He'll have questions for you when you arrive.

"Did you serve me? Did you stay true to your wife? Did you keep faith with your kids? If you messed up, did you take all possible steps to make things as right as possible? Did you repent? Did you start over again?"

Live the kind of life that, once finished, moves God to say, "Well done, good and faithful servant. Enter into the joy of your Lord."

The Great Male Bonding Weekend

G. Ron Darbee

"He jumps! He shoots! He scores!" I screamed as the miniature sponge basketball sank through the net hanging from the living room door. A few victory laps around the coffee table, index fingers extended, and a chant of "I'm number one! I'm number one!" provoked my son into an unflattering bout of poor sportsmanship. (Where do kids pick up this stuff?)

"You cheat!" he yelled.

I took a quick glance over each shoulder, convinced he was addressing someone else.

"I'm sorry. Were you talking to me? I know you weren't talking to me," I said, "because if you were, you would have addressed me with respect. You would have called me by a name suitable for someone of my advanced athletic stature. Something like 'Champ' or 'Hoopster,' maybe even 'Grand Master of Roundball.'" I felt another victory lap coming on.

"You shoved me and your hand was in my face! You can't do that!"

"I out-played you, Son. I simply applied a little pressure under the net, and you folded. It's called technique."

"It's called cheating."

"Hey, you say tomato . . ." I paused for effect. "I'll tell you what. We'll make it best-out-of-three, but then Jake takes the winner." Jake was on the couch, laughing hysterically or suffering from some sort of violent convulsions. Either way, the boy obviously wasn't used to witnessing healthy communication.

"Is your dad always like this?" Jake asked.

"Only when we miss a dose of his medication," Ron answered. "By the way, don't leave anything sharp lying around."

This was day two of our "bachelor weekend." The women in our lives had abandoned us in favor of a mother/daughter retreat. Since Jake's mom was a single parent, he joined Ron and me to complete our "Three Musketeers." Actually, had his mother believed for a moment that Jake would eat anything *besides* Three Musketeers, he might have stayed home alone. But as it turned out, he stayed with us. We were glad to have him, and we needed the referee.

"You know, I've worked up quite a thirst with all this celebrating," I said. "What say we hit the kitchen and grab some refreshments." Two teenagers bolting from the room produced a refreshing breeze, and I followed along in their draft.

"I'll get the milk," my son said.

"I'll get the glasses," Jake offered.

"Stop, hold it right there," I said. "Boys, you obviously don't understand the finer points of a bachelor weekend. Allow me to explain. Rule number one: Toilet seats are to remain in the raised

position. Rule number two: There is no distinction between hand towels and dish towels. And number three: No glasses. We drink out of the cartons."

"How come?" Ron asked.

"Because we can. Now each of you mark a carton with your name. I don't want your nasty little lips on my milk carton."

Sprawled across the living room floor, drinking from our individual cartons, we passed the time with a little conversation. The subjects of sports, cars, and, or course, sports cars having been exhausted the day before, the boys chose to educate me on a proper masculine image.

"Nothing personal, Mr. Darbee," Jake said, "but don't you think this whole bachelor weekend thing is kinda lame?"

"Define lame," I said.

"Well, you know, like weak, senseless."

"I'm not following you."

"What he means, Dad," my son joined in, "is if you're the man of the house, why do we need all these rules for a bachelor weekend? You're in charge, right? Why can't we do all this stuff when Mom's around?"

"Mom, there are three open milk cartons in the refrigerator, and they all have lip prints on them."

"I get it," I said. "What you're trying to say is I'm the king of the castle, lord of the manor, that sort of thing."

"Right," Jake said.

"Things will be different when I'm married," Ron said. "If I want to drink from the carton or eat with my hands, I will. Nobody's gonna tell me what to do. Besides, it's biblical."

"Biblical?" I questioned. "Please, share with me the source of your scholarly knowledge."

"It's Ephesians 5:22," Jake said. "We read it in Sunday School last week. 'Wives, submit to your husbands as to the Lord.'"

"I see. And this you chose to memorize. I mean with all the Scripture at your fingertips, this is the verse that spoke to your hearts?"

"Yeah," they responded.

"OK. I think I understand the problem," I said, picking up a Bible to use as a visual aid. "This is the Word of God, gentlemen, not a fortune cookie. You cannot read one verse and apply it at your convenience. Read verse twenty-five."

Ron took the Bible and turned to Ephesians 5. "Husbands, love your wives, just as Christ loved the church and gave himself up for her," he read.

"And would that indicate, then, that some personal sacrifice might be necessary on your part?" I said.

"Can we get back to you?" Jake asked. The boys left the room to reevaluate their position.

Late that afternoon, the women returned home, signifying an end to our bachelor weekend. Always the perfect gentleman, I held the door as the ladies carried in their luggage.

"Mom, there are three open milk cartons in the refrigerator, and they all have lip prints on them," my daughter announced, inspecting the contents for any other sign of violation.

"I can explain that, dear," I told my wife.

"Well, you know how I love a good story," my wife said, "but wait just a minute and I'll be back. It was a long trip."

As my wife left the room, our son suddenly remembered a

problem. "Oh yeah, Dad. The light's out in the bathroom. I think it needs—"

"Eeeeeeyaaah" *Splash!* The scream cut him off in mid-sentence.

"What do you say we head over to the school and shoot some hoops?" I said. "Or would you boys care to share that memory verse with your mothers?" Ron rushed to find the basketball. Jake had kissed his mother and was already out the door.

"Melissa, hand this to Mom, and tell her we'll see her later. And welcome home, Sweetheart."

"But this is a dish towel," she said.

"That's OK. It's an emergency."

The Uncivil War

Dave Meurer

The battle had been looming for weeks. My flight date had been set for well over a month, and Dale had been glumly marking off each day on the calendar.

"I'm going to miss you," she said.

"I'll miss you, too," I replied.

But a man's gotta do what a man's gotta do.

War is always so hard on the women who are left behind.

I kissed Dale good-bye and boarded the flight. Several hours later I touched down in Memphis, Tennessee. The weather was typical southern summer fare, and within moments my clothes were sticking to my back.

It was an unlikely group of guys who composed our unit. In civilian life, I was an aide to a member of Congress. Michael had just wrapped up a semester at the University of Tennessee, where he engaged in some heavy-duty computer work for the

Department of Defense. He would be tasked with recording the devastation on videotape, which would be painstakingly analyzed again and again and again after the heat of battle was over.

Tim, our unit leader, worked as a substance-abuse counselor at a leading Memphis hospital. His colleagues had no clue about the double life he led.

Scott was a financial analyst for a British-owned company with a keen interest in penetrating the American market. He had been tasked with much of the acquisitions work. A not insignificant amount of money had been allotted to weaponry.

A sixth sense told him that he would suffer massive collateral damage.

John was the wild card. With substantial training in hand-to-hand combat, his participation was critical, though he was harboring serious reservations about the operation. But he was in too deep to back out now—a fact that Tim reminded him of on more than one occasion.

By the following afternoon, the quiet suburban home that served as our command center would be a flurry of activity as plans were finalized and weapons were checked and rechecked.

Tim reviewed the staging area—three long boards laid across two saw horses—and nodded approvingly at the array of ammunitions: a huge bowl of instant mashed potatoes (dyed green for added effect), two dozen partially melted chocolate fudge cookies, a massive vat of pork and beans, four dozen generic cans of soda, several twenty-four-ounce squeeze containers of French's yellow mustard—and that was just for starters.

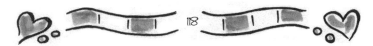

Clearly, this would be the biggest food fight in Memphis history—and quite possibly the most heated battle the South had seen since the Union Army hammered Sherman's forces with the strategic but historically obscure surprise attack of lime Jell-O salad (with raisins).

Complicating the battle would be the presence of the mercenaries—numerous youngsters ranging from first-graders to high-schoolers. Their allegiance shifted on a minute-by-minute basis depending on which side produced the most interesting ammo.

"I think I'll just watch y'all have fun," said John, as Tim scooped two gallons of off-brand Neapolitan ice cream into a large pan, where it wilted under the fierce summer sun.

"I think you won't," Tim grinned in reply.

John's concern was quite understandable and quite warranted. The first food fight, conducted the prior summer, had been a far less lethal affair with only four participants and far more modest munitions. John's military training told him that this second battle would be a brutal, take-no-prisoners operation, where a likely key target would be the only retired member of the United States Marine Corps, who happened to be the father or grandfather of roughly half the assembled forces and who, hands down, presented the largest target available. A sixth sense told him that he would suffer massive collateral damage. His premonition would be proved uncannily correct.

A seemingly inexhaustible supply of wickedly gooey groceries— foodstuffs that were never intended to share the same table, much less be hurled through the air at high speeds—were conveyed from the kitchen to the backyard, where the makeshift table groaned with the weight of it all.

Two dozen raw eggs floated in a green Tupperware bowl. A mess o' grits, left over from breakfast, provided an important statement about southern solidarity, and were apparently reserved for the poor schlep from California. (The author is convinced he was set up for the grits because he refused to eat them earlier.)

The ketchup, Cool Whip, bananas, and five-pound sack of Pillsbury unbleached flour filled out the basic ammo checklist. The six plastic bottles of root beer served as the food fighter version of weapons of mass destruction. With a small hole jabbed by an ice pick into the lid, the two-liter bottles (after a savage shaking) would emit an impressive stream of foaming fury that could reach a good fifteen feet.

The troops gathered merrily around the table amid John's stern warning to "LEAVE THE TABLE ALONE UNTIL THE 'BEFORE' PICTURE IS SNAPPED!" As the group of combatants smiled for the camera, they failed to notice John's massive paw reaching into the ice cream. The shutter clicked just in time to forever record the look of shocked surprise on Tim's face as a pint of frigid, multicolored dessert began oozing down the inside of the backside of his swim trunks.

Pandemonium erupted. The actual battle defies description. Imagine standing inside a gigantic food processor that is being fed by a deranged Julia Child and the image will be pretty close.

Grits spattered my face as I flung a glob of green potatoes in a retaliatory strike. A flurry of black-eyed peas pelted John as he peppered Scott with a particularly lethal barrage of diced peaches (in heavy syrup). John then slipped on a strategically placed banana and was immediately smothered by a generous represen-

tation of all the major food groups wielded by squealing, soda-drenched grandchildren.

The cold war doctrine of Mutual Assured Destruction was fully embraced by all sides. The air was a fog of hideously incompatible ingredients all randomly detonating on all targets.

There was no strategic defense, no "umbrella of protection" to ward off the incoming volleys of yams and globs of peach Jell-O. There was, however, a dizzying number of shifting alliances, double-crosses, and Machiavellian strategies—all formed and abandoned within seconds of what turned out to be a seven–minute war. Sort of like the State Legislature moments before it wraps up the final budget bills.

And the moral of the story is simply this: if you visit the South, you ain't leavin' until, one way or the other, you have tried some grits.

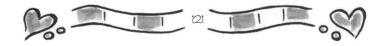

Tales of Mischief
Phil Callaway

"The best way to keep children home is to make the home atmosphere pleasant—and let the air out of their tires."
—Dorothy Parker

Tonight, after scolding the boys for feeding birthday candles to a neighbor's dog, I chase them to bed snackless, then sit in the living room, wondering if there's any hope at all for my descendants. "Do you ever wonder," I ask Ramona, "what will happen to a generation that doesn't even know which way to wear their hats? A generation raised on Nintendo and microwave hot dogs? I mean, seriously . . . sometimes I wonder what the world will be like when all the prayer warriors are gone. When all the great preachers and writers and missionaries have passed off the scene."

"I sometimes worry about the kids," admits my wife. "Because, well, honey, they're a lot like you."

Thankfully the phone interrupts our conversation.

The caller is a friend I haven't seen in years. Would I care to join him and a few others for a friendly game of floor hockey? Now, please understand that at my age (38), when you are just grateful for the strength to rise unaided from the sofa and waddle to the kitchen for six square meals a day, one should not entertain thoughts of dashing up and down the gym floor trying to prove himself a teenager. But there's no way I'm admitting it. Quicker than you can say cardiac arrest, I say yes.

By the end of round one my face is roughly the color of a ripe plum. "I think I pulled some fat," I tell my teammates. By the end of round two I have contracted a respiratory problem and, unable to find an oxygen tent, I suggest that we retire to my house for a healthy snack, namely Pepsi and chips. The suggestion is welcomed by Dave Wall and Pete Rashleigh, two childhood buddies, and soon we're sitting around the table swapping tales of mischief and laughing until my respiratory problems return.

The three of us grew up in a conservative community where we worked hard to make a name for ourselves. Unfortunately, the names some grown-ups called us are not safe to print. Here is a short list of our exploits to help you understand why (please do not let your children see these):

1. Using dark felt pens to add a single consonant to garage sale signs so that they read "Garbage Sale."
2. Sneaking into the church nursery and placing limburger cheese in diapers.
3. Calling the morgue to inform them that Mr. Amstutz, our tenth grade math teacher, was dead.

We also tell tales of Super-Gluing salt shakers to restaurant

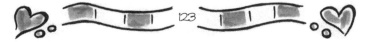

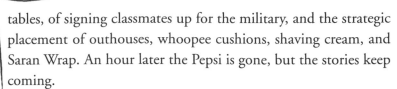

tables, of signing classmates up for the military, and the strategic placement of outhouses, whoopee cushions, shaving cream, and Saran Wrap. An hour later the Pepsi is gone, but the stories keep coming.

"Most of the stuff we did you couldn't put in print," admits Dave. "My teachers hated me. Every time I turned around they spanked me. You check the dictionary for 'brat' and you'll find my high school picture."

Pete's list of accomplishments rivaled Dave's. "I was chased by security guards, banned from talent shows, and kicked out of Bible college . . . and that was during one of my better weeks," he says. "I used to steal tapes from Christian record stores."

The clock slips past midnight before we grow quiet . . . and a little more serious. Pete shakes his head. "On countless nights my parents lay awake wondering when the police would call. And praying for the day I'd come home."

Dave nods his head. "Same here."

On Pete's twentieth birthday, God got his attention. "I was going eighty miles an hour on a motorcycle when we crashed," he says. "I was lying in the ditch unconscious and I had this dream where everything was pitch black. When I woke up this guy was standing over me, his lips moving rapidly. He was praying. That was the day I gave up running. And came Home for good."

Today Pete is senior pastor of a Baptist church. He just named his firstborn daughter Karis—Greek for grace. And Dave? Well, he's quit taunting his teachers, and joined them. When he isn't playing practical jokes on the natives, he teaches the Bible to a remote tribe in Papua, New Guinea.

Pete and Dave know a few things for sure. They know that God has a great sense of humor, that He loves nothing more than

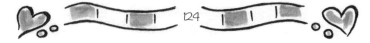

watching wandering boys come Home, and they'd tell you any-time that their lives have never been more exciting than they are right now.

The clock is moving toward one as I bid them good night. The children are asleep, so I slip silently into their rooms, place a soft hand on their heads, and pray. *Dear God, thank You that there is hope, after all. That You delight in changing people. Will You do as much for my kids? Will You take their energy, and shape it for good? May they find in me something worth imitating. And may they find in You everything they'll ever need to make a mark on this old world.*

On the way to bed, I switch off the kitchen light and pull aside a curtain. Sure enough. Pete and Dave are still parked in the driveway, the hood up.

I guess they haven't found the potato I put in their exhaust pipe.

Fishing Diary

Dave Meurer

Day 1

The key to successful fishing is to be named Walt.

I learned this today when my friend Dan and I brought to Oregon's Umpqua River every conceivable item of fishing gear produced by Western civilization in the past several centuries—including neoprene waders, an array of lures more expensive than the crown jewels of France, and even fashionable T-shirts with fishing logos—but the only guy who caught a fish was Walt.

He was using some cheap plastic round thing that only a complete moron of a fish would mistake for a salmon egg, but steelhead fled from our $5.95 Mepps lures like they were toxic waste and lunged instead at Walt's glob of plastic as though it were the last morsel of food on the planet. If the average steelhead is stupid enough to fall for Walt's inexpensive treachery,

then everything *Field & Steam* has ever published is a filthy lie. The editors just realize that the day they run a story titled "Only Guys Named Walt Will Catch a Fish" is the day they sell their last magazine. But now their little secret is out.

Walt insists that the real key to fishing is abandoning all personal hygiene for the duration of the trip. He says filth "covers up" the human scent. We believe he is just trying to keep us from scampering down to the courthouse to have our names legally changed to "Walt."

Day 2

Today I learned that plunging into the freezing Umpqua River is something you probably want to avoid, especially when you have your outlandishly expensive Nikon camera slung around your neck. Although I demonstrated that this is a bad idea, Dan insisted on trying it himself. Bear in mind that we are both *paying* for this experience. Walt, on the other hand, escaped unscathed. The disturbing "Walt Trend" thus continues.

Dan and I are increasingly suspicious.

We made Walt sleep near an open window tonight.

Day 3

Another member of our fishing excursion, Lyle, has landed a salmon the approximate weight and dimensions of Winston Churchill. He was not using Walt's cheap plastic egg, and he also regularly brushes his teeth. And, tellingly, he was not sporting a fake "Hi! My name is Walt" name badge like Dan and I were.

While this breaks the disturbing Walt Trend, it also blows my initial theory regarding why I have caught nothing. Perhaps my

fishing logo T-shirts are insufficiently attractive to our prey. Tomorrow I shall boldly switch to a forest green sweatshirt emblazoned with the words "Catch and Release." This may convince them that I mean no harm. In reality, I have already purchased a substantial quantity of mesquite briquettes and cleaned the ashes from my Weber.

Inasmuch as Lyle is a minister, I have taken the opportunity to probe deep theological questions, such as: "Since Jesus called His followers to become 'fishers of men,' wouldn't it be considered moral laxity for a minister to leave that high calling and become a mere fisher of fish?"

He said I can't have his salmon, and that if he catches me near his ice chest again he will phone the authorities. Clearly, I have touched a raw nerve and he is wracked with guilt.

Meanwhile, Walt is violating federal clean air standards each time he raises his arm to cast.

Day 4

Dan and I groused to the lady at the tackle shop about our bad luck. She suggested we try a "Dupont Spinner" which, she chuckled, is a euphemism for dynamite. We asked what aisle it was in, and she grew serious and said she was just joking and then made disparaging comments about our sportsmanship. What a cruel hoax.

Dan is growing particularly edgy and has purchased sixteen additional fashionable T-shirts, which he changes every few minutes. Lyle is basking in the glow of success, and Walt is wearing a halo of flies. We make him fish WAY downwind of us.

Dan and I must pack our bags and go home tomorrow to face the ridicule of defeat. At least it isn't just me getting skunked.

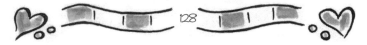

Tail End of Day 4

Dan has landed a steelhead the size of an apartment complex.

He was not wearing a fishing logo T-shirt at the time. And he was using a four-pound test line, which is akin to dragging a submarine to shore with dental floss.

The key to successful fishing is not to be named Dave.

Maybe I'll go try that "fisher of men" thing that Lyle keeps talking about. It doesn't require special T-shirts, it is less smelly, and if you succeed you don't even have to gut anything.

Up in Smoke

Phil Callaway

If you bump into the average person on the street, chances are good that they will have heard of recycling (chances are that they will sue you, too, but that's another chapter). Though most humans are familiar with recycling, few know who invented it.

Allow me to set the record straight.

It was the summer of my tenth birthday. A picture-perfect summer, framed with barefoot fishing trips and sleeping beneath the stars. My friend Gary and I established The Gang of Two that summer. I'm not sure if you ever heard of us. But early each morning after our fathers went to work, we borrowed their shovels and spent the day burrowing deep into the bowels of the earth. I, Captain Phil, pretty much gave orders. Private Gary pretty much followed them.

Each day—thanks in large part to Gary's unwavering obedience —we burrowed a little deeper. Each day, by 5 p.m., we returned

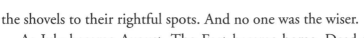

the shovels to their rightful spots. And no one was the wiser.

As July became August, The Fort became home. Dead tree branches camouflaged her from the onslaught of rival gangs. Tall weeds concealed her inhabitants from passersby. In those weeds we sat, decked out in imaginary khaki outfits, imaginary guns in hand, launching surprise attacks on passing cars, which were Nazi U-boats and sometimes tanks.

Then one morning in mid-August, after dying theatrically from a U-boat torpedo, Gary spoke the fatal words: "I'm bored."

As captain, it was my job to turn such words into adventure, so I quickly responded, "What say we stop saving The Fort and start saving The Earth?" The thought was a new one for both of us, which was why Gary pushed aside two large flowered weeds, looked at me with his head to one side, and said, "Huh?" But once I explained my plan, it made perfect sense.

That afternoon, as the hot summer sun beat mercilessly through the ozone layer and danced on the asphalt around our feet, we put our plan to work: we purged the main street of our little town of every visible cigarette butt.

GARY (picking up another one): "Boy, are these ever disgusting!"

ME (loudly, in the direction of the curious passers by): "Yes, Gary. Put 'em in the bag and we'll throw 'em in the trash!"

GARY (with a loathing look): "To think people actually smoke these things!"

Upon completion of our task, we carried the butts to our headquarters in the woods and concluded The Plan: we recycled them, one by one. Right down to the filters.

In fact, we recycled pretty much anything we could get our lips around that summer. Tea leaves. Cinnamon. Dried dandelions. Pencil shavings. Newspaper. Cardboard. You

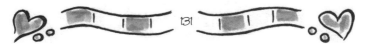

name it, we sat in the weeds and inhaled it.

I believe it was a Wednesday that completely changed our lives. Gary approached me on his bicycle, breathless. "You ain't agonna believe this," he said, throwing himself on the grass, rolling in the suspense of it all.

"Okay, let me guess. Um, it's gotta be candy. Your mom bought you all you can eat?"

"No, better."

"Uh, she bought you a motorcycle?"

"Nope," he said, unable to contain his excitement any longer. "I found A PACK OF 'EM. It ain't even been opened."

"Naw, you're lyin'."

But he wasn't lyin'. In fact, carefully concealed in the tall shadow of an obscure telephone pole was proof: Player's Filter Tip, unopened and beckoning.

She was standing outside the restroom, wondering who had established a tobacco plantation on her property.

Now I knew the punishment for smoking. My older brother had told me all about it. "They cut your lips off," he said. So, casting anxious glances in all directions, we stripped off the plastic and divided The Pack evenly. Ten apiece. And we smoked them. One by one. Right down to the filters.

As our time behind the pole drew to a close, we pooled our wisdom and experience, noting what scientists would later discover: anything that tastes this bad can't be too good for you. Or, as Gary put it so eloquently, "These things are awful. Let's never ever as long as we both shall live touch another one." After shaking tobacco-stained hands on it, I suggested, somewhat deliri-

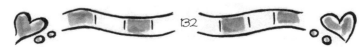

ously, that we get home and, furthermore, that we do so quickly, maximizing the time needed to re-enter the non-smoking zone.

"Hmmmm," sniffed Gary's mother. "What's that smell?"

Half an hour had passed, and she was standing outside the family restroom, wondering who had established a tobacco plantation on her property without securing permission. Gary crouched in the bathtub, caught yellow-handed. "I, uh, was smoking," was all he could say. But I was older than Gary. I was wiser. I knew that as ye smoke, so shall ye reek. So, in an effort to keep the consequences of my own sins at bay, I slipped silently through our back door and up to the medicine cabinet. From there, I tiptoed to my room, concealing a can of spray deodorant and a full tube of toothpaste. After lengthy attention to personal hygiene, I was finally able to approach my parents. "Hmmmm," sniffed my father. "You sure smell nice, Philip."

Later that evening I crawled into bed, a satisfied smile stuck to my face. *Boy, are you ever brilliant,* I thought. *No one will ever know.*

Mom entered my room then, opened the window and sat on the bed. "Did it taste good?" she grinned.

"Uh . . . whaa . . . supper? Oh, yes, Mom it was very good. Thank you."

"When I was a girl," she continued, "my grandpa let me smoke his pipe. I didn't like it . . . How about you?"

"Me neither, Mom," I said, closing my eyes. Then I stuck out my lips because I knew the punishment.

She could have cut my lips off. She could have at least spanked me (this had been done before), or quoted Scripture. She could have reminded me that nothing we do will ever be hidden from God. That no amount of toothpaste or deodorant will cover our sins. That they really will find us out. She could have

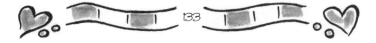

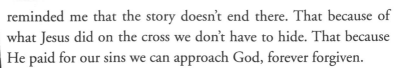

reminded me that the story doesn't end there. That because of what Jesus did on the cross we don't have to hide. That because He paid for our sins we can approach God, forever forgiven.

Instead, she leaned over and kissed me squarely on the forehead.

"I'll never smoke again," I said.

Then, "Mom, how did you know?"

She grinned again. "Well, son, sometimes ten-year-old boys forget that their mothers have friends, too."

From the bathroom my father hollered: "Hey, has anyone seen the toothpaste?"

6

Friends: Can't Live without 'Em!

Complete Strangers

Be kind to your friends. Without them
you'd be a complete stranger.

—Lowell D. Streiker
A Treasury of Humor

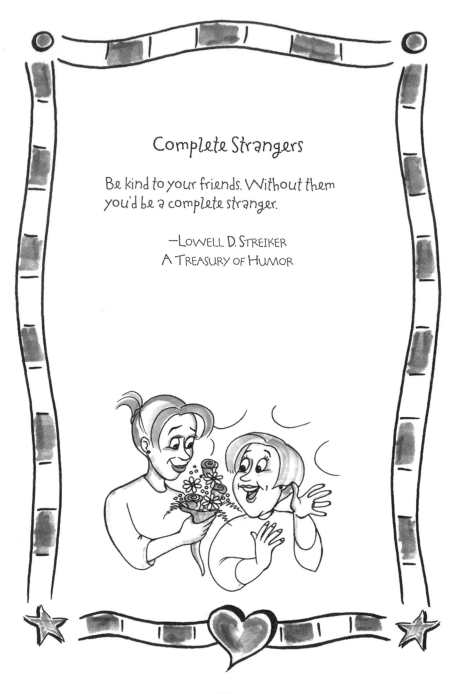

There's No Friend like a Sister

Tina Krause

Pam and Beth's hectic schedules made it nearly impossible to schedule a day in which they could buy their mom a joint birthday gift, especially during the holidays. On their only day off, they met at the mall one afternoon to try to find the perfect gift. But everything that could go wrong did, and time was slipping away.

Frustrated and anxious, they pressed through the crowd; then, at the same moment, a store advertisement caught their eyes. It read: "ONE DAY ONLY . . . EVERYTHING OFF!"

"That's for sure!" both exclaimed aloud, thinking how "off" their one day had been. Instantly, they burst into laughter and their stress diminished.

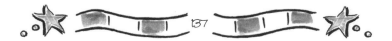

No Woman Is an Island

Karen Scalf Linamen

There's a certain camaraderie among women.

Whether we're talking about the attitudes of our kids, the contents of our refrigerators, or the girth of our waistlines, we members of the sisterhood of women just seem to have a lot in common.

Maybe it's because we battle so many of the same problems.

Last week I was visiting my folks in Colorado. My mom and I were puttering around together in the kitchen when she said, "Wanna know the best piece of advice I ever got from you?"

Now, I don't normally go around giving advice to my mom—she's a lot wiser than I am—so I was interested to hear what she was about to say. Maybe she had been impressed with some profound insight she'd picked up from something I'd written or while she and I were having an intimate conversation on some deeply spiritual topic.

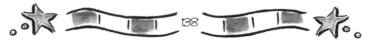

She said, "It was when you told me to soak crusty pans overnight in automatic dishwashing soap. I haven't scrubbed a pot since."

It's true. If you have a pot or pan with baked-on goo from supper, just fill it with water and toss in some Cascade. The pan wipes clean in the morning.

See? That's what I'm talking about. We all face so many of the same challenges. Whether we're single gals or empty nesters, newlyweds or midlife moms, we all know what it's like to try to scrape the remains of last night's lasagna off our favorite CorningWare.

I love it when another woman shares some little tidbit from her own life—an experience or insight—and it's something I've experienced or thought, but figured I was the only one.

I loved it, for example, when a reader wrote to me and confessed that she sometimes cleans her house and then realizes that lurking in the back of her mind is the motivating thought, barely acknowledged, that once her house is clean someone—she doesn't really know who—will arrive at her home and rescue her from all of her troubles. And my eyes blinked wide as I read, and I laughed out loud in amazement.

I thought I was the only one who had experienced that sensation.

I love it when I go to my friend Beth's house. We've been friends for four years now. Not just friends. Close friends. Bosom buddies. And in all our many hours together, I've never once visited her home and used the bathroom frequented by her kids and found the roll of toilet paper ON THE DISPENSER. Not a single time. And I love it because I can relate. In my bathrooms, entire generations of toilet paper rolls will come and go without

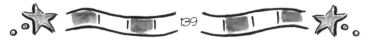

ever having been introduced to the dispenser next to the toilet. It's as if the dispenser has been relegated to the roll of some antiquated appliance that once served a purpose, but has fallen into disuse, like the twenty-pound waffle makers we all used to own or the toaster oven or the rotary dial phone.

But somehow knowing that the dispenser has fallen into disuse at Beth's house makes me feel a little better. Less guilty. I may still get the Bad Mother of the Year Award for letting my kids manually unwind their own toilet paper, but at least I won't be making my acceptance speech all alone. Beth'll be right beside me, sharing the podium.

I think one of the scariest feelings in the world is wondering if you're all alone. Of course, I realize that mothers of preschoolers may take issue with this statement because the thing they crave even more than chocolate is isolation. This is because these women have not experienced a private moment—not even to go to the bathroom—since the birth of their first child. But I'm not talking about THAT kind of alone. I'm talking about the alone we feel when we're afraid everyone else is living Martha Stewart/Ruth Graham lives while *our* lives resemble something more akin to Lucy Ricardo meets Roseanne Conner. At Peyton Place, no less.

But that's the nice thing about having friends with whom to share the intimate details of our lives. It helps us realize that we're ALL living Lucy/Roseanne/Peyton Place lives.

King Solomon had it figured out. He wasn't even a woman and he had it figured out (of course, he WAS married to seven hundred of them, so maybe that helped him get a clue). I say he had it figured out because he's credited with writing, in the Book

of Ecclesiastes, the observation that "there is nothing new under the sun."

And there isn't.

So the next time you're feeling like no one could possibly understand the things you're going through, think again.

I don't know about you, but I think this is comforting, not because "misery loves company," but because "there's strength in numbers."

And not just strength. There's hope, too. Because if other women have experienced the same struggles and emerged victorious to tell the story, then you and I can do it, too. Although I have to admit, I'm more than a little curious how Solomon's wives made do with baked-on lasagna.

Planes, Trains, and Laughter

Luci Swindoll

A couple of years ago Marilyn Meberg and I spoke on Mackinac Island, off the coast of Michigan. We got stranded due to bad weather. In order to catch our plane on time, we had to take a horse and buggy, boat, taxi, and bus. Literally! At every juncture it seemed one more thing went wrong. We might have worried ourselves into a very bad mood or complained and made our displeasure known to all who crossed our path. We could have had a miserable day. We certainly had all the ingredients to make us out of sorts. But we were together; and there was absolutely nothing we could do to improve our lot in life, for that day anyway. So we decided to make the most of the adventure. Having made such a good decision as that, we had the time of our lives. We've looked back on that day as one of the most memorable times of spontaneous fun we've ever enjoyed in our long friendship.

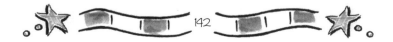

All along the way during that very unpredictable day, we played a ridiculous game. "Hey, Mare," I said, "they say we'll miss the boat because of the fog, but I don't think we will. I'll buy you breakfast if we do." She came back with a snappy retort: "You little optimist. Of course we'll miss the boat. If we don't, breakfast is on me." She bought breakfast.

Later, it was obvious the taxi would not be waiting in the designated spot. "Hey, Mare," I said, "they say we'll arrive too late to catch the bus, but I don't think we will. I'll buy you lunch if we do." Marilyn responded, "You silly girl. Of course we're going to miss the bus. Look at your watch. If we don't, lunch is on me." She bought lunch.

And so the day went just like that. We were in a pickle for sure. But somehow, our experience was delightful. In the end, we got home without a hitch. I was very full and Marilyn, very poor. She'd picked up the tab for all three meals and every snack. Actually, it was very cheap entertainment for us both. And we laughed ourselves silly.

It's all in the attitude. Once we learn to capture these unexpected moments of surprise and potential disappointment, an even greater spirit of adventure is born in our hearts.

Quack, Quack

Karen Scalf Linamen

Last night Beth and I went out for coffee. She's in the middle of remodeling her bathroom and was feeling stressed with her husband and kids and the plumber and the tile man and just pretty much life in general.

So we ended up in a booth at Chile's.

We scanned the menu, ordered two cups of coffee, the tuna fillet and grilled veggies, then went back to discussing Beth's stress and the fact that she was down to her last nerve.

Little did we know that our waiter was about to find that last nerve and walk all over it.

It started when he brought coffee, sugar, and cream but no silverware.

Beth spent the next five minutes trying to wave him down. After she asked for silverware, he brought forks but no spoons.

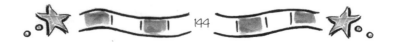

Another five minutes passed as Beth tried to get his attention. When she did, she growled, in a voice reminiscent of Linda Blair's in *The Exorcist*, "We'd like some SPOONS here." He apologized and promptly brought us two long-handled iced tea spoons that would have made it possible for us to stir the coffees of the couple sitting four booths away.

By now I was trying hard not to laugh, and Beth was trying hard not to make headlines in the next morning's paper: "Waiter in Critical Condition after Being Bludgeoned by Spoon-Wielding Midlife Mom."

I looked across the table at my friend. "I have three little words that will save you."

She asked, "What are they?"

I said, "Be a duck."

She said, "Excuse me?"

I said, "A duck. Be one. Okay, close your eyes. Take a deep breath. Visualize with me. You're a duck. The clueless waiter is a drop of water. He falls on your feathers. He rolls right off. Water off a duck's back and all that. You're not even wet. Let it go, Beth. Let it roll right off. Take a deep breath and let it go. Be a duck. Say 'I'm a duck.'"

She closed her eyes and said, "I'm a duck."

(See why I love my friends?)

I said, "That's right. Be a duck. Be a duck. Be a duck."

She opened her eyes and flashed me a wicked grin. "You know, this is going to come back to haunt you the next time you're upset about something."

I laughed. "I know. And when my turn comes, don't worry. I'll be a duck, too."

I love figuring out new ways to cope with the stresses and messes of life. When life hurts, what helps? Indeed, my last two books have been dedicated to answering that very question— each book contains more than a dozen tried-and-true ways to feel better when life throws you a curve.

Although I have to admit, the duck speech came out of the blue. It was a new one even for me. But I think it helped, and I'm definitely going to try it myself the next time I feel my blood start to boil.

> I love figuring out new ways to cope with the stresses and messes of life.

I wish you and I were immune to crisis, but unfortunately we're not. Emotional crises, family crises, health crises, beauty crises, even trainee waiter crises—we're subject to them all, aren't we?

Not long ago, however, I experienced a crisis even I wasn't prepared for. It was a crisis of faith. I'm writing about this because last week I got a letter from a woman named Deborah who wrote, "I've been living on antidepressants for the past year and am struggling with my faith."

And I could really relate, because a couple years ago I found myself in a lot of emotional pain, and somehow, in the process, my faith took a real beating as well.

Now, I've met folks and I'm sure you have, too, who—when crisis comes a callin'—say, "My faith is the thing that got me through."

One of my girlfriends was like this. Jenny was diagnosed with

breast cancer at 32, brain cancer at 35, and was a citizen of heaven by 37. But in the meantime, everyone who loved her got to watch her faith grow into something massive and muscled and strong, an Arnold Schwarzenegger–sized faith, and it was a beautiful thing to see.

In MY times of crises, however, my faith becomes an eighty-pound weakling that couldn't get me out of a soggy paper sack.

Not all the time. But more often than I like to admit.

I'm happy to say, however, that the thing that gets me through—even when my faith is knock-kneed and anemic and in need of an awful lot of handholding and antibiotics and maybe even CPR—isn't a thing at all but a Person.

A couple years ago I was in such emotional pain that I was having a hard time walking with the Lord. To be honest, I wasn't even trying. And when it came to prayer, the best I could muster was a single plea, and for months these were my only words to God, and they went like this:

"Lord, hang on to me. I know I should be hanging on to you, but I'm not. The truth is, I feel too wounded and broken and angry and rebellious and hurt right now to hang on to you. So if I'm going to get through this at all, it's got to be up to you. See me through this, Lord, hang on, please hang on to me and don't let go."

And guess what?

He hung on.

When life hurts, what helps? The list is long: laughing, crying, counseling, working out, music, insightful sermons, caring friends, gardening, whining, praying, reading, reflecting, and even quacking come to mind.

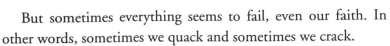

But sometimes everything seems to fail, even our faith. In other words, sometimes we quack and sometimes we crack.

Even then there's hope. Because even when our faith's not strong our God is faithful.

Daisy, Daffy, and Donald don't know what they're missing.

Joy to the World

Susan Duke

As soon as we spied the first guests turning into the driveway, Judy and I ran out onto her charming Victorian porch, positioned ourselves audaciously on the top two steps, and began joyfully belting out the "Hallelujah Chorus."

"Hallelujah, hallelujah . . . Hallelujah! Hallelujah! Hal—leee—lu—jah!"

We were a bit off-key, but we didn't care. The grins and giggles from the ladies getting out of their cars only heightened our spirited enthusiasm. What a sight we were: two forty-something women dressed up in homemade angel attire, complete with puffy wings of white tulle and sparkly, golden halos. Our guests stared, staggered, and sashayed their way up the red-brick path leading to Judy's front porch, their faces registering everything from utter shock and dismay to bubbling jubilation.

"We're your heavenly hostesses today!" we declared as we ushered each lady inside to our second annual After-Thanksgiving Tea, a special party for all the women in our family and their invited guests. The house smelled of spiced tea, freshly baked sugarplum cake, and cranberry candles. Judy's dining table was set with her best dishes, finger sandwiches, and all the trimmings for an elegant and delectable lunch.

I suppose the women weren't all that surprised to see Judy and me dressed up as angels. They knew we are both little girls at heart. In fact, people have always commented on how much Judy and I are alike. Her mother and mine were expecting us at the same time. I was born in June; Judy, in July. The fact that her father was my half brother made me her aunt when I was a mere one-month-old! We had fun growing up together and have remained close through the years. Sometimes our eyes still twinkle just like they did when we were giddy four-year-olds stirring up delicious mud pies enriched with sugar, cinnamon, and Kool-Aid!

> I suppose the women weren't all that surprised to see Judy and me dressed up as angels.

The After-Thanksgiving Tea was Judy's idea. Thanksgiving is our designated family-reunion time, with the traditional meal usually served at Judy's parents' house. Each year Judy and I wait until the family has feasted on turkey and the men are all comfortably positioned in their armchairs for an afternoon of football. Then we sneak away to her house a few miles down the road. That's when we catch up on each other's lives over a cup of hot tea and simply while away the afternoon in her old porch swing.

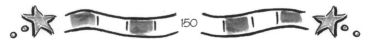

But for several years, sitting on Judy's front porch, we found ourselves asking each other the same question: "Why can't Thanksgiving be different? It's great being with family; but all we do is eat, go our separate ways, and it's over. Where's the meaning? The tradition? The spiritual and emotional bonding?"

It troubled us.

Then, as another Thanksgiving approached, Judy called me. "Suzie, I've had a brainstorm," she said. "I know what we can do about Thanksgiving this year! You'll have to help me pull it together, but I think we can do this."

"What are you talking about?" I asked.

"You know how we've longed for Thanksgiving to be different—to have more meaning and tradition? Well, I've been thinking. If it's ever going to be different, we're going to have to be the ones to change things. We've been waiting for someone else to do something, but we're the ones who love making memories and encouraging people. So maybe *we're* the ones who should start a new tradition.

"What do you think about having a tea party at my house the day after Thanksgiving for all the women in the family?" she continued excitedly. "They can even invite guests. I'll prepare a variety of finger sandwiches, vegetable dips, and desserts. We'll exchange small gifts, and I'll give a devotional. You can sing and read us one of your stories. Won't this be a wonderful way to start the Christmas season?"

"It sounds great," I said, "but it also sounds like a lot of work for you. Besides, do you think anyone will actually come? We'll be competing with the after-Thanksgiving sales!"

"Suzie, it really doesn't matter how many women show up. We need this—and everyone else does too. They just don't know

it yet! I think an after-Thanksgiving tea party will encourage our families to be closer and give us something to look forward to. So how about it?

Of course, I couldn't refuse. Judy was right. We had griped and complained for years. Now, instead of remaining a part of the problem, we could be part of the solution.

My daughter, Kelly, Judy's daughter, Amanda, and Judy's sisters, Cindy and Loretta, agreed to help with the party. That first year we were thrilled when close to thirty enthusiastic family members and friends showed up. The laughter and tears we shared were a dream come true for Judy and me. A fresh tradition had been birthed.

The next year I was the one with the brainstorm. Judy and I had already decided that the theme for the second annual tea would be angels. Everyone would bring an angel gift or ornament to exchange. But then another idea came to me.

Just a few days before Thanksgiving, I called Judy long-distance. "I know something that will perfectly complete the theme for our tea this year," I said excitedly. "Since you and I are hosting, we can dress up as 'heavenly hostesses'—you know, in angel outfits!"

"Oh, Suzie, you've got to be kidding," Judy objected. "I'm so busy getting everything ready at my house, I don't have time to find angel outfits!"

"Don't worry. I'll gather up all the stuff," I promised. "I don't know how yet, but by Thanksgiving, I'll have our heavenly attire ready."

"Girl, I don't know about this," Judy laughed. "But I'm game if you are!"

I'm constantly amazed at the way God takes one little idea and turns it into a small bit of heavenly manna to be shared with

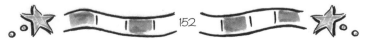

others. For instance, I never expected what happened at the local Wal-Mart Supercenter when I went shopping for our angelic apparel. After I found some white sheets, I selected a roll of white bridal tulle from the fabric department and asked the lady at the cutting table to measure and cut six yards.

"Someone getting married?" the fabric clerk asked.

"No ma'am," I replied.

"Well, I've noticed that people are using this stuff to wrap baskets and make bows. It does make great bows, doesn't it?

"I wouldn't know. I've never made bows with it," I said.

"Well, I'm sure there are all sorts of things you can use this stuff for—potpourri sachets, dish scrubbers, and who knows what."

I'm amazed at the way God takes one little idea and turns it into a small bit of heavenly manna.

The inquisitive lady obviously wanted to know why I was buying six yards of white tulle. I just wasn't sure I was brave enough to tell her.

Finally she asked me outright: "Well, what *do* you plan on doing with this stuff?"

"Actually, I'm going to try to make some angel wings," I admitted.

"Oh? Is one of your children in a play?"

"No, as a matter of fact, *I'm* going to be the angel."

The fabric clerk's dark red eyebrows sprang up like two tightly rolled window shades, and her eyes shouted, *Lady, are you for real?*

Feeling I owed her some sort of explanation at that point, I told her about the family tea party and the angel theme. A few

moments later her eyes began to glisten, and soft tears trickled down her ruddy cheeks.

"I'm sorry. I don't know why I'm crying," she said. "This just sounds like such a wonderful idea! I have three sisters in town, and we never get together anymore. We used to be close, but after our mom died a few years ago, we sort of drifted apart. I've been wondering lately how I could reach out and show them how important it is for us to be close again. You've inspired me to call them and invite them over for a tea party."

She wiped her eyes. "You just don't know how this has made my day! In fact, it's beginning to feel like Thanksgiving to me for the first time in years!"

A few days later I arrived at Judy's house, angel costumes in tow. We had such fun getting ready—we made a precious memory even before the tea began! We giggled like kids playing dress-up, fluffing our wings, shaping our halos, and lacing up our tennis shoes (which we made sure *weren't* covered by our robes). Judy wore red high tops, and I wore my white Reeboks—part of the uniform for fast-running angels, we reasoned. Judy's angel name became Holly because her last name is Wood and she wanted to be Miss Hollywood. Mine was Leon, which is *noel* spelled backward—since backward is the direction I'm apt to be flying most of the time. We thought we'd been close before; after that morning, we were celestially bonded!

> A few moments later her eyes began to glisten, and soft tears trickled down her ruddy cheeks.

Our mothers, daughters, sisters, aunts, nieces, and cousins came to the tea, and everyone had a wonderful afternoon. Each woman got her picture made with the angels. The photograph of my mom and me is framed and sits where I can see it even now as I type. Another one of Judy and me chasing each other around a tree reminds me that the kid in both of us is still alive and well. May we never get too old or too staid in our ways to be a little bit silly!

As it turned out, our angel costumes got quite a workout that day. When all the guests had gone home, Judy's sister Cindy asked us to go to the hospital in our angel garb to visit a cousin who hadn't been able to take off from work that day. We agreed—but only if she'd dress up and go with us. So the three of us, in all our homemade glory, along with a few other relatives, piled into a Jeep and drove to the hospital. The strange looks we got at red lights and again when we entered the hospital made us wonder if someone might call security on us!

We packed into an elevator and pushed the sixth-floor button. On the way up, however, the doors opened on the second floor. A lady waiting there for the elevator took one look at us—and screamed.

"Fear not!" I said as the doors closed again in front of her.

By the time we got to the lab where our cousin Jackie worked, we were so giddy we were afraid we might get thrown out of the hospital. But Jackie, who laughed and thanked us for coming to see her, had plans for us. She knew a couple of special patients who needed cheering up—and she was sure three angels were just the thing to do it.

In fact, one of the patients was a sixteen-year-old girl named

Sarah, who loved collecting angels. She was just coming out of a coma after a serious automobile accident. As we appeared at her bedside and sang "Hark! The Herald Angels Sing," we could see her sweet eyes silently telling us "thank you." Several months later Sarah called Judy to let her know that she was finally home and doing fine—and that she'd always remember the real-life angels who came to sing to her in the hospital. Her mother also got on the phone and told Judy that she could never express how much joy our visit had brought at such a critical time in their family's life.

In another room we sang to a man who had only weeks to live. He laughed at the mere sight of us! He loved to laugh, his wife told us. So we asked him to sing along with us on a special rendition of "Hark! The *Hairy* Angels Sing." He was still laughing out loud when we left the room. His wife followed us outside, grabbed our hands, and with tear-filled eyes thanked us over and over for the visit.

Funny what a couple of sheets and a few yards of tulle can do! When I shared the pictures from the tea party with a friend back in my hometown, she asked me to put on the angel outfit once again and go with her to visit a friend who was in dire need of cheering up. She brought her own homemade cardboard wings, and we trotted off on our angel mission of mercy. That's a whole other story that would take too long to tell. But I will tell you this—thinking about it makes me want to sing the "Hallelujah Chorus" all over again!

Everyone needs an angel sometimes. And I've learned something new since I first took that flying leap into angel territory. *Real* angels have their work cut out for them! They certainly don't need the help of daring, fun-loving impersonators, but it's awe-

some to see what God can do with a little imagination! To be a pretend angel, even for a little while, was a joy unlike any I think I've ever experienced. It's one of those ideas that happen to turn out right—and one that keeps on making my heart smile.

C. S. Lewis once wrote, "Joy is the serious business of heaven." My angel wings and I agree. That's why I keep them hanging in my closet, just in case I'm called to active angel duty again. For I've learned a valuable truth over the years: joy shared brings a double blessing. Opportunities to spread a little cheer in this world are heaven's mandate—and earth's reward.

Unexpected Delights

Luci Swindoll

On the morning of August 11, 1991, I went to my friend Mary's home for breakfast. As she was setting the table, I broke my left leg. I don't usually do this sort of thing, but I was having such a relaxing time puttering around on her patio, watering and pruning a few plants. In my effort to pull a loose branch off a big fern (we are talkin' *really big* here, folks; the fern that ate L.A.), my feet flew out from under me and I hit the pavement with a splat. I could swear I heard the bone break. You don't want me to describe the sound.

Not knowing the extent of the injury, Mary took me to the emergency room at a nearby hospital where I was admitted, x-rayed, and told I had a six-inch break in the fibula, just above the ankle. (That's the smaller of the two bones that runs between the knee and the foot.) I was offered the choice between having no surgery (but wearing a cast from toes to groin

for eight to twelve months) or having a metal plate with six or seven screws surgically inserted in the break area, which would help me heal in only four months. I chose the latter option.

Well, what an interesting four months those were! First of all, my orthopedic surgeon, Dr. Michael Kropf, turned out to be young, good-looking, gentle, and tremendous fun. Even when he changed my initial cast by sawing it off with a vibrating blade and I got a look at my swollen, bruised leg for the first time, he was very tender. He even permitted me to include Mary, who at my request took pictures of the whole procedure. (She got a little queasy, but I did just fine.)

On the third day after the fall and my release from the hospital, I made a conscious decision about the coming months. I wasn't going to let my broken leg, my cast, or my crutches get in the way of my life. In fact, I wrote in my journal (and I quote), "I'm not going to let this stop me. I'll look at every day as a challenge and watch the Lord make the crooked places straight. He knows my need, and he'll meet me there." And did he ever!

There were numerous occasions during that time of healing when he delighted me with his faithfulness. In spite of my broken leg I went to work every day, to Colorado on vacation, and to Italy for Marilyn's daughter's wedding. I never missed a single speaking engagement in six different states.

The most wild experience, however, was early in December when I flew to Chicago where I was to change planes for the Twin Cities. It was very cold and snowing in Chicago when I was met at my gate by an American Airlines attendant with a wheelchair. When he wheeled me over to board my connecting flight, the word "canceled" was flashing on the screen. "Is this flight to Minneapolis–St. Paul *really* canceled?" I asked in all seriousness.

"Indeed it is, ma'am," he replied. "That airport is shut down, and nobody is flying in there today. Sorry."

I asked to be pushed over to a pay phone, where I called my hostess in Minneapolis to report what had happened. "Oh, Luci," she said, "I called you this morning to tell you not to come, but you had already left. I feel so bad that you made this trip for nothing."

Well, as it turned out, it wasn't for "nothing" after all. When I explained my plight to the guy pushing my wheelchair, he smiled sweetly and asked, "May I take you to lunch? Then we'll get you on a return flight to California. Would that be okay?"

Later that evening, I invited a few friends over for pizza. As we were each discussing the events of our day, they asked sympathetically, "And what did you do today, Luci, being in a wheelchair and all?" I *delighted* in telling them I had flown to Chicago for lunch!

Each of us has something broken in our lives: a broken promise, a broken dream, a broken marriage, a broken heart . . . and we must decide how we're going to deal with our brokenness. We can wallow in self-pity or regret, accomplishing nothing and having no fun or joy in our circumstances; or we can determine with our will to take a few risks, get out of our comfort zone, and see what God will do to bring unexpected delight in our time of need.

Ernest Hemingway puts it this way in *A Farewell to Arms:* "The world breaks everyone and many are strong at the broken places." I challenge you to be one of the many. Take that step of faith and ask God to surprise you in a unique way that only he has the flair to accomplish.

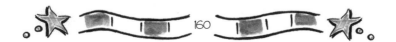

There's Such a Thing as Too Much Encouragement

Karen Scalf Linamen

Beth is not only a very good kidnapper, she makes a mean casserole to boot.

One day she dropped by to cheer me up. She brought with her this heavenly casserole. I mean, this casserole was amazing. It had tons of cheese and sliced eggplant and some eggs and tons of cream, and it had this Mediterranean-flavor thing happening, and it just melted in your mouth, and it was truly wonderful.

I get sort of passionate about food, if you hadn't noticed.

Anyway, so Beth shows up on my doorstep, and I make us some coffee, and we dig into her casserole, and we spend several hours just talking about life in general and my life in particular. It was nothing short of a Kodak moment, all the encouraging and bonding and feasting that was occurring.

Early afternoon, I walked her to the door. She paused on my front porch, and our conversation began meandering toward

good-byes. We chatted casually about nothing in particular, when suddenly I announced, "I'm going to make it."

Beth said, "I KNOW you're going to make it. You're strong. You're a wonderful person, and you've gone through some tough times but, yes, you're going to make it. And I'm going to be there with you every step of the way. No matter what the future holds, no matter what decisions you make with your life, I love you and I'll be there for you. You're going to be okay, Karen. This year is going to be a new chapter in your life. You're going to be fine. You really ARE going to make it."

By now there were tears in her eyes.

I blinked. I stared. Then I said, "I meant the casserole."

"The casserole?"

"I meant I'm going to make your casserole."

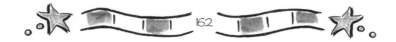

Friends You Can
Count On

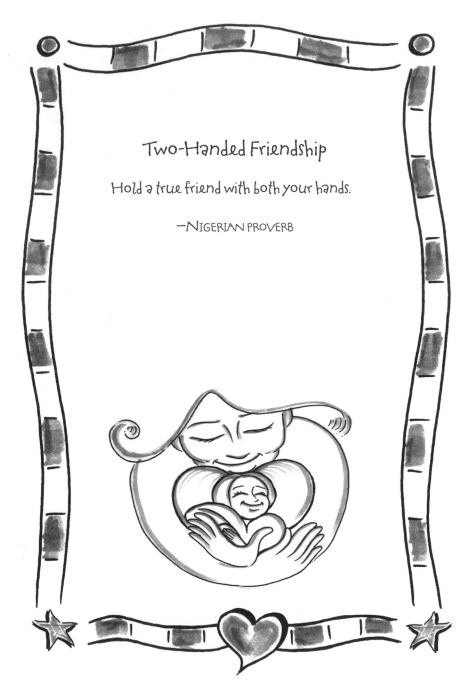

Two-Handed Friendship

Hold a true friend with both your hands.

—NIGERIAN PROVERB

I've Only Got Eyelids for You

Martha Bolton

My good friends Linda Aleahmad, a licensed marriage and family therapist, and Mary Scott, a poet and administrative assistant to a Southern California newspaper editor, and I celebrate our birthdays together each year. We usually go out to a nice restaurant and talk about things like life, work, children, and of course, growing older. No matter how much we don't want to be reminded of it, the subject of aging almost always comes up, and we spend the rest of the evening comparing our latest physical changes and laughing about them as much as possible.

Tonight the physical change du jour was droopy eyelids. Each of us noted that our once perky eyelids had recently unperked themselves, and as Joshua might have said at the wall of Jericho, "They've come a tumbling down!" Not that we're tripping over them or anything, but they've drooped enough to give us that

half-open, half-closed look that so many of us had through high school and college.

It seemed to happen to each of us overnight. Eyelids are sneaky that way. You go to bed with all your body parts exactly where they're supposed to be: Chin in place? *Check.* Lips in place? *Check.* Eyelids where they're supposed to be? *Check.* But when you wake up in the morning and look in the mirror, you notice that the rest of your body is exactly where it was eight hours ago, but your eyelids are now drooping like Deputy Dawg's, and you're just about as excited as he is about it.

I suppose we shouldn't be surprised. Our eyelids can't be expected to stay at attention forever. Forty or fifty years is long enough. They're pooped. They're ready for a break. They've faithfully served at their post and now they deserve a rest.

Unfortunately, though, their early retirement begins to place undo pressure on the eyelashes. They are the only things between the avalanche of flesh and our cheekbones.

A business associate of mine had her eyelids pulled back surgically. That's one solution, I suppose. And yes, it worked, but now she has that wide-awake look, like someone just said, "Boo!"

My friends and I spent the evening together weighing the pros and cons of getting our eyelids done but decided against it. We opted to keep the skin we're in and let nature take its course. We would be thankful for our health, our families, and all our blessings. It seemed like the right thing to do—especially when we remembered that Thanksgiving was just around the corner.

I think there was something about my neck that reminded them.

If I Should Die Before I Wake... Call My Friend

Sue Buchanan

Peggy knows exactly what to do if I should die suddenly. She has her orders! Before my body is cold, she's supposed to nose around, see that I've left this earth in an orderly fashion, and take care of anything that might be left undone.

For instance, I'd want her to make sure there's nothing disgusting growing in my refrigerator, like rotten lettuce or moldy cheese, unless by chance I'm in the middle of an experiment like maybe growing my own penicillin.

Peggy would know instinctively that I wouldn't want a dirty cup or glass in the sink, and she'd know to slice a lemon and run it through the disposal to give it a fresh smell. If they should carry me out feet first and the bed wasn't made, she would make it.

I'd want her to look around for anything that might embarrass me, like the dirt under the big kitchen rug. When I cook I kick crumbs and crud under it to be dealt with at a later time.

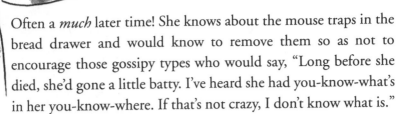

Often a *much* later time! She knows about the mouse traps in the bread drawer and would know to remove them so as not to encourage those gossipy types who would say, "Long before she died, she'd gone a little batty. I've heard she had you-know-what's in her you-know-where. If that's not crazy, I don't know what is."

There's a perfectly logical explanation for the you-know-whats in the you-know-where! Several years ago we discovered telltale traces of mice in our bread drawer. We spoke to our two cats about it and they assured us (mostly by their blank looks) that had these sneaky little rodents set foot in *their* kitchen, they would have known about it and acted immediately, if not sooner. From that we concluded the mice had "broken and entered" through the back of the bread drawer.

With an "I'll fix them," I headed straight to the hardware store, bought traps, and put them in the bread drawer. I intended to go back later and set them. (Would you leave your mouse traps sitting out in plain sight? I don't think so.) Perhaps just the sight of the traps scared the mice back into the woods. I never set the traps and never saw the mouse mess again.

Thank heavens for Peggy. She would fix things and I could rest in peace, knowing I'd covered all my bases here on earth. Having my bases covered for the hereafter is quite another thing! I'm thankful that God didn't have to make arrangements as elaborate as mine when he planned for our eternal destiny. He only asked us to accept that his Son Jesus paid the consequences for our sin and to live our lives in gratitude and obedience. What could be simpler?

Death Doesn't Become Us

Martha Bolton

Since my friend Mary had recently attended a family funeral, the subject moved from fallen eyelids to funerals, wills, and last wishes. Linda was the first to share what she wanted done with her remains.

"I want to be cremated," she said, "and my ashes placed inside a firecracker and shot into the air in one spectacular sendoff."

We figured it must be the cheesecake gone to her head.

Mary said she wanted to be cremated, too, but she also wanted a memorial service in which people said nice things about her. She also wanted a good picture on display, and she'd like her ashes scattered in the barranca in Ventura, California.

I opted for a more traditional funeral. I want nice things said about me at my funeral, too (I'll write them up ahead of time), but I also want the service to be full of funny remembrances. I've embraced laughter my entire life. I wouldn't want it to be missing

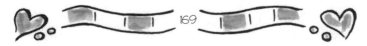

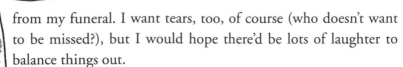

from my funeral. I want tears, too, of course (who doesn't want to be missed?), but I would hope there'd be lots of laughter to balance things out.

I also asked them to help my husband with the telephone calls. I know him too well. He'll have every intention of calling all my friends listed in our telephone book, but he won't make it past the C's. It'll be wearying to keep relating the same story over and over again, reliving all the details of how I left this world—especially if I go in some bizarre way like "The manager at the skating rink said it was the first time they'd ever lost anyone during the Hokey Pokey, but they're still going to award her the free CD posthumously for all her efforts." Or "We told her not to use the computer while in the bathtub, but she just mumbled something about a deadline, plugged it in, and deleted herself. We tried to save her as a text file, but we got there too late."

However it happens, my husband will get tired of telling the same tale again and again, so he'll just quit—right after the C's. My friends whose last names begin with the letters D through Z won't find out about my demise until I'm missing from the family-photo Christmas card. I can hear the phone calls now.

"Where's Martha? I didn't see her by the tree."

"Oh, didn't you know?" my husband will say. "She passed on six months ago."

"Why didn't anyone tell me?"

"I would have, but you weren't in the front of the phone book."

The Comfort of Friends

Barbara Johnson

Someone told me that her favorite Scripture verse was, "And it came to pass." I looked at her rather quizzically, and then she laughed and added, "Just think. All this could have come to *stay!*" While we are in the passing-through stages, we have to derive comfort from others who have survived. Be a survivor, and help someone else!

Cornbread: The Stuff of Friendships

Cathy Lee Phillips

It was a way of life. From time to time some of my dearest animal friends made the transition from pasture to freezer.

As the child of a farm family, you quickly learn not to become too attached to what will eventually become your meatloaf or pot roast. Nevertheless, some animals are unforgettable!

There was Beetlebomm the bull, a close friend who ate apples from my hand. There was Tootey-Belle, the three-legged calf who could outrun any other animal in the pasture. And, who could forget Ed the pig, famous for his habit of jumping out of the pen and chasing cars. They were a unique collection of characters, certainly, and there was cause for mourning when their fateful day arrived. Nevertheless, those days were inevitable and the table was abundantly filled during the following weeks and months.

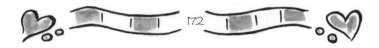

It was during one of those weeks that Vicky and Dan Anderson dropped by one Tuesday evening just before dinner. Their timing was perfect! Our home was decorated with the addictive odors of pot roast and homemade biscuits. As they were seated, it was obvious that Vicky and Dan were not leaving and they, in fact, responded quickly to Mama's dinner invitation. The evening was relaxing and enjoyable—so much so that the next evening, just before dinner, Vicky and Dan returned. Mama, being the wonderful hostess, was calm as she quickly thawed T-bones under hot running water. The dinner was delicious, Vicky and Dan said as they were leaving soon after dessert.

We were really surprised at seeing the Andersons two nights in a row. Even more surprising, though, was watching their now-familiar car turn into the driveway the following evening.

Vicky and Dan loved the pork chops on Thursday, the fried chicken on Friday, and the ham on Saturday. It was quite obvious that a pattern had developed that left my mother planning and cooking dinner for eight people. She decided to fight back!

Sunday arrived and, with it, Vicky and Dan. They walked into the kitchen and found my mother preparing cornbread.

"That's one of my favorites!" Dan bellowed as he seated himself at the table.

"I'm so glad," my mother responded, placing the cornbread and a huge bowl of pinto beans in the middle of the dining room table. She seated herself silently and moved only to butter her cornbread.

"Oh no," I groaned to myself, having a great hatred of pinto beans and cornbread. "Surely there is more on the way."

But there wasn't. Dan's smile faded as he silently partook of

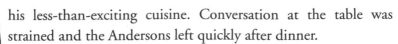

his less-than-exciting cuisine. Conversation at the table was strained and the Andersons left quickly after dinner.

As I helped Mama clear the table, I asked, "Do you think they will be back tomorrow night?"

"Oh, I hope so," she smiled slyly, "we still have quite a few pinto beans."

Vicky and Dan did not return the next night nor the night after that. In fact, it was a very long time before we saw them again.

But that's okay because I learned a great lesson from them.

Pot roast friends are fine.

But help me, O Lord, to be a cornbread friend!

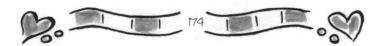

Love in a Bear Suit

Susan Duke

The saying is true: A picture *is* worth a thousand words. The surprised look on Joanna's face, followed by a smile as wide as Texas, can only be described as indescribable.

She had no idea when she opened her front door that night what was about to take place.

Nor did I.

Earlier in the day, Joanna had called me with bad news. She'd been to the doctor, and her latest results showed the cancer she'd been battling for more than a year was still raging. The chemotherapy and radiation had done little to hold it at bay. For the first time since her diagnosis, I heard—through sobs and broken sentences—hopelessness and fear in my dear friend's voice. Until now, she'd been full of faith and high spirits.

But today was different.

I prayed with her before we hung up, but afterward, I cried. Slow, silent tears.

"How can I help Joanna, Lord?" I prayed in desperation. "How can I encourage her, minister to her, give her hope? Please show me what to do."

I called two other close friends—Janice and Brenda. With Joanna, we were the "Steel Magnolias." That's what Joanna's husband, Robert, called us, explaining that our friendship reminded him of the friends in the popular 1989 movie. The four of us live an hour apart in opposite directions and don't get together all that often, but we stay in touch, praying for each other and pulling together when there is a need.

"Janice, have you talked to Joanna yet?"

"Yes, we just hung up," Janice said.

"Do you plan on going to see her tonight?"

"Yes. I was thinking about taking supper over there for her and Robert. If you and Harvey come, I'll get my Charlie to come too. I'll bring enough food for everybody. When you call Brenda, tell her not to eat beforehand if she can join us."

"Okay," I agreed. "I'll call Brenda at work in a few minutes. I keep feeling that we need to do something really special for Joanna—something different—to lift her spirits. I know we can go and visit, pray, and take them supper, but how can we make Joanna smile again?"

"I don't know," Janice replied. "But let me know if you think of something."

I waited before I called Brenda to tell her the plans, hoping God would give me an idea. *What will make Joanna smile?*

From out of the blue, a wild idea formed in my mind.

"Lord, surely this isn't You planting this kind of thought in my head! I know You work in mysterious ways, but I'll have to pray about this some more!" I said out loud.

But the thoughts and ideas continued to flow—so much so that I finally dialed Brenda's work number to run my idea by her.

Her response didn't surprise me.

"You're going to do *what?* Are you sure this idea is the Lord's doing?" she laughed.

"Well, I *think* it is," I said. "I know it sounds crazy. I thought so too. But I can't get away from thinking about what it might do for Joanna."

I waited, hoping God would give me an idea. What will make Joanna smile?

"But, Susan—a *bear suit?* You've got to be kidding! Where in the world could you even find one to rent?"

"Well . . . I was thinking you could help me out since I'm here in the boonies and you're in the big city of Dallas."

"Oh, please!" Brenda objected. "I can't find you a bear suit. I've got work to do! Besides, who would I call?"

"A costume shop. Just ask if they have a teddy bear suit for rent," I coaxed. "As wild as it seems, I think this is divinely inspired! Joanna needs something special—a memory she'll never forget—to let her know we love her so much we'd do almost anything to make her laugh again. Tell me you don't think I'm crazy!"

"You're crazy!" Brenda laughed.

"I knew you'd say that! But can't you see it? We'll have a

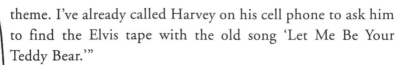

theme. I've already called Harvey on his cell phone to ask him to find the Elvis tape with the old song 'Let Me Be Your Teddy Bear.'"

"Okay, *if* I can find you a bear suit to wear, and Janice brings the food, what should I do?" Brenda asked.

"How about getting Joanna a cuddly teddy bear and some colorful balloons?" I suggested.

"That sounds good. Let me see if I can find this bear suit, and I'll call you back."

Thirty minutes later my phone rang. It was Brenda.

"I can't find a bear suit anywhere in Dallas," she said. "I've found gorilla suits, rabbit and dog suits, but no bear suits! So now what? Are you sure this is a God thing?"

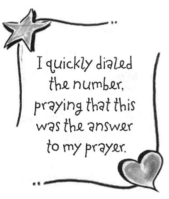

I quickly dialed the number, praying that this was the answer to my prayer.

"Well, I guess we'll know soon enough," I responded. "If there's no bear costume in Dallas, I'm sure there's nothing out here in the boonies. But I'll try the surrounding towns."

I pulled out the phone book with listings from several adjacent counties and searched the yellow pages under C for a costume shop within thirty miles. Lo and behold, I found one in my very own town!

I quickly dialed the number, praying that I wasn't totally off my rocker and that this was the answer to my prayer.

"Hello," I said. "I was wondering if you might by chance have a bear suit."

"Well, as a matter of fact, we do," the shopkeeper answered without hesitation.

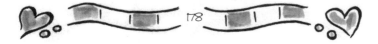

I was so shocked, I asked again. "You do? You *really do* have a bear suit—not Smokey the Bear or a grizzly bear, but a *teddy bear* suit?"

"Yes ma'am, we surely do."

"What is your overnight rental fee?" I asked, still incredulous.

"One hundred and twenty-five dollars," the shopkeeper said.

"You're kidding, right? I don't want to buy it—just rent it for a few hours."

"That's our rental fee," the woman answered firmly.

Now what? I thought. *I can't afford to spend that much! Even if the girls went in with me, that's still a lot of money just to wear a bear suit for thirty minutes.*

My heart sank. "I'll have to get back with you," I told the lady on the phone. "I really wanted to do something special for a friend who's going through a very tough time, but this is way out of my budget."

I was about to hang up when the woman began to ask me a few questions about Joanna. "I can tell you're disappointed about this bear suit," she said finally. "And I've never done this for anyone before, but how about renting the suit for half the price I quoted you?"

"Oh my! Are you sure? This will be such a blessing to my friend," I gushed. "Thank you so much! I'll pick it up within the hour." I wanted to leap like a kid when I got off the phone—and I couldn't wait to call Brenda back.

"You're never going to believe where I found a bear suit!" I shouted. "Practically in my own backyard. See, this must be God!"

We both laughed as we finalized our plans for the evening. We'd meet at Joanna's house at six-thirty. I'd have my portable cassette player in hand, cued to start playing Elvis's "Let Me Be

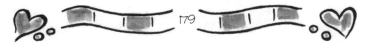

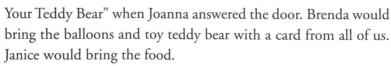

Your Teddy Bear" when Joanna answered the door. Brenda would bring the balloons and toy teddy bear with a card from all of us. Janice would bring the food.

Once we arrived, Harvey had to help me out of the car because the huge, furry bear head almost filled the entire front seat. He put our dog's leash around my neck so he could lead me up to the house.

Everyone converged on Joanna's front porch. Charlie, Janice, and her cousin Susie carried armloads of food in containers; Brenda was partially hidden behind a mass of purple and yellow balloons; and Harvey had his hands full trying to keep me from tripping over my twenty-four-inch bear paws.

We rang the doorbell. Silently, I prayed that we were doing the right thing.

Joanna turned the doorknob.

Elvis started singing!

I grabbed Joanna's hand, and we jitterbugged around the room. She giggled like a child and fell onto the couch laughing and holding her sides. When she regained her composure, she read the friendship card and a poem I'd written for her called "Tough Bear."

As she hugged the plush teddy bear Brenda had brought, the tears came.

"Y'all are too much!" she cried. "I can't believe you did all this for me. I could never forget this in a million years. I don't know when I've laughed so hard."

That night we feasted, prayed together, and embraced God's gift of laughter. As someone once said, "Laughter is the closest thing to the grace of God." God Himself says in Proverbs 17:22 that laughter is like medicine.

Yes, a picture really is worth a thousand words. And if, through the pain and adversities of this life, our hearts can remember the portraits of laughter we've shared with friends, we'll have been given a precious gift: a glimpse of heaven here on earth.

Source Notes

Chapter 1: Friendship Means Never Having to Say You're Embarrassed

"A Friendly Reminder" taken from *Amusing Grace* by Rhonda Rhea. Copyright © 2003. Used by permission, Cook Communications Ministries.

"Burping to Bond" taken from *I'm Not Suffering from Insanity . . . I'm Enjoying Every Minute of It!* by Karen Scalf Linamen. Copyright © 2002. Used by permission, Fleming H. Revell, a division of Baker Book House Company.

"The Giddies" from *Laughter Therapy* by Tina Krause, copyright © 2002, published by Barbour Books, an imprint of Barbour Publishing, Inc., Uhrichsville, Ohio. Used by permission.

"Move Out!" taken from *Amusing Grace* by Rhonda Rhea.

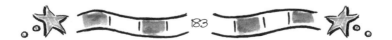

"Girlfriend Day '95" taken from *Gutsy Little Flowers* by Cathy Lee Phillips. Copyright © 2001 by Patchwork Press, Ltd. Used by permission.

"Love Me, Love My Mess" from *Laughter Therapy* by Tina Krause, copyright © 2002 published by Barbour Books, an imprint of Barbour Publishing, Inc., Uhrichsville, Ohio. Used by permission.

Chapter 2: Friends Come in All Shapes and Sizes

"The Spirit Is Willing, but the Dentures Are Missing" taken from *The Buzzards Are Circling, but God's Not Finished with Me Yet.* Copyright © 2001 by Stan Toler. Used by permission, Chariot, Victor. All rights reserved.

"A Few Good Guys" taken from *Who Put My Life on Fast-Forward?* Copyright © 2002 by Phil Callaway. Published by Harvest House Publishers, Eugene, OR 97402. Used by permission.

"Junior Friends" taken from *Fresh Elastic for Stretched Out Moms* by Barbara Johnson. Copyright © 2003. Used by permission, Fleming H. Revell, a division of Baker Book House Company.

"Of Love and Friendship" from *Lessons for a Super Mom* by Helen Widger Middlebrooke, copyright © 2002, published by Barbour Books, an imprint of Barbour Publishing, Inc., Uhrichsville, Ohio. Used by permission.

"Man's Best Friend" taken from *Abba's Child* by Brennan Manning, copyright © 2002. Used by permission of NavPress—www.navpress.com. All rights reserved.

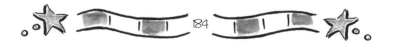

"Shhh . . . Jesus Is in the Room" taken from *Aging, Ailments, and Attitudes* by Cathy Lee Phillips. Copyright © 2003 by Patchwork Press, Ltd. Used by permission.

"The Hug Is Sharper Than the Sword" taken from *Nothing Builds Togetherness like Wrestling for Remote Control* by G. Ron Darbee. Copyright © 1996. Used by permission, Broadman & Holman.

Chapter 3: Of Friends and Kids

"You Know There's a Baby in the House When . . ." taken from *Who Put the Pizza in the VCR?* by Martha Bolton. Copyright © 1996 by Martha Bolton. Published by Servant Publications, P.O. Box 8617, Ann Arbor, MI 48107. Used with permission.

"Annual Letter" by Lynn Bowen Walker. Used by permission.

"The Red Jell-O Caper" taken from *Fresh Elastic for Stretched Out Moms* by Barbara Johnson. Copyright © 2003. Used by permission, Fleming H. Revell, a division of Baker Book House Company.

"Baby-U" taken from *Who Put the Pizza in the VCR?* by Martha Bolton. Copyright © 1996 by Martha Bolton. Published by Servant Publications, P.O. Box 8617, Ann Arbor, MI 48107. Used with permission.

"I Once Was Lost" taken from *Nothing Builds Togetherness like Wrestling for Remote Control* by G. Ron Darbee. Copyright © 1996. Used by permission, Broadman & Holman.

"A-flat" from *An Owner's Guide to Fatherhood* by Chris Ewing, copyright © 2000, published by Promise Press, an imprint of Barbour Publishing, Inc., Uhrichsville, Ohio. Used by permission.

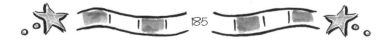

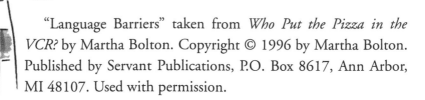

"Language Barriers" taken from *Who Put the Pizza in the VCR?* by Martha Bolton. Copyright © 1996 by Martha Bolton. Published by Servant Publications, P.O. Box 8617, Ann Arbor, MI 48107. Used with permission.

Chapter 4: Friends through It All

"Friendship Is Blind" taken from *Seeing Beyond the Wrinkles* by Charles Tindell. Copyright © 1999. Used by permission, Studio 4 Productions, Northridge, CA.

"Girl Talk" taken from *Welcome to the Funny Farm* by Karen Scalf Linamen. Copyright © 2001. Used by permission, Fleming H. Revell, a division of Baker Book House Company.

"With Nuts or Without?" taken from *Through the Rocky Road and into the Rainbow Sherbet* by Laura Jensen Walker. Copyright © 2002. Used by permission, Fleming H. Revell, a division of Baker Book House Company.

"Make a Friend . . . Again" taken from *I'm Not Suffering from Insanity . . . I'm Enjoying Every Minute of It!* by Karen Scalf Linamen. Copyright © 2002. Used by permission, Fleming H. Revell, a division of Baker Book House Company.

"Sistership" taken from *The Best Devotions of Patsy Clairmont* by Patsy Clairmont. Copyright © 2001 by Women of Faith. Used by permission of Zondervan.

"With Friends like These" by Luci Swindoll taken from *Joy Breaks* by Barbara E. Johnson, Patsy Clairmont, Luci Swindoll, and Marilyn Meberg. Copyright © 1997 by New Life Clinics. Used by permission of Zondervan.

"Don't Look at Me" taken from *I Wonder What Noah Did with the Woodpeckers* by Tim Wildmon, copyright © 1999 pub-

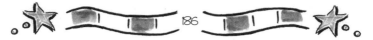

lished by Promise Press, an imprint of Barbour Publishing, Inc., Uhrichsville, Ohio. Used by permission.

Chapter 5: Real Men Do Have Friends

"Craziness Loves Company" excerpted from *Who Put the Skunk in the Trunk?* Copyright © 1999 by Phil Callaway. Used by permission of Multnomah Publishers, Inc.

"Geezer Guys" taken from *Stark Raving Dad!* by Dave Meurer. Copyright © 2002. Used by permission, Bethany House Publishers.

"The Great Male Bonding Weekend" taken from *Nothing Builds Togetherness like Wrestling for Remote Control* by G. Ron Darbee. Copyright © 1996. Used by permission, Broadman & Holman.

"The Uncivil War" taken from *Out on a Whim* by Dave Meurer. Copyright © 2001. Used by permission, Bethany House Publishers.

"Tales of Mischief" taken from *Who Put the Skunk in the Trunk?* Copyright © 1999 by Phil Callaway. Used by permission of Multnomah Publishers, Inc.

"Fishing Diary" taken from *Out on a Whim* by Dave Meurer. Copyright © 2001. Used by permission, Bethany House Publishers.

"Up in Smoke" taken from *I Used to Have Answers, Now I Have Kids.* Copyright © 2000 by Phil Callaway. Published by Harvest House Publishers, Eugene, OR 97402. Used by permission.

Chapter 6: Friends: Can't Live Without 'Em!

"There's No Friend Like a Sister" taken from *Laughter Therapy* by Tina Krause, published by Barbour Books, an

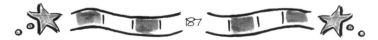

imprint of Barbour Publishing, Inc., Uhrichsville, Ohio. Copyright © 2002. Used by permission.

"No Woman Is an Island" taken from *Welcome to the Funny Farm* by Karen Scalf Linamen. Copyright © 2001. Used by permission, Fleming H. Revell, a division of Baker Book House Company.

"Planes, Trains, and Laughter" taken from *I Married Adventure*, by Luci Swindoll, copyright © 2002, W Publishing, Nashville, TN. All rights reserved. Used by permission.

"Quack, Quack" taken from *Welcome to the Funny Farm* by Karen Scalf Linamen. Copyright © 2001. Used by permission, Fleming H. Revell, a division of Baker Book House Company.

"Joy to the World" taken from *Earth Angels* by Susan Duke. Copyright © 2002. Used by permission, Howard Publishing Company.

"Unexpected Delights" taken from *The Best Devotions of Luci Swindoll* by Luci Swindoll. Copyright © 2001 by Women of Faith. Used by permission of Zondervan.

"There's Such a Thing as *Too Much* Encouragement" taken from *I'm Not Suffering from Insanity . . . I'm Enjoying Every Minute of It!* by Karen Scalf Linamen. Copyright © 2002. Used by permission, Fleming H. Revell, a division of Baker Book House Company.

Chapter 7: Friends You Can Count On

"I've Only Got Eyelids for You" taken from *Didn't My Skin Used to Fit?* by Martha Bolton. Copyright © 2000. Used by permission, Bethany House Publishers.

"If I Should Die Before I Wake . . . Call My Friend" taken

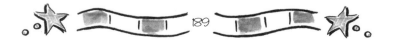

Contributors

Martha Bolton is a former staff writer for Bob Hope, two-time Angel Award recipient, Emmy nominee, and the author of more than thirty books, including *Didn't My Skin Used to Fit?* and *Who Put the Pizza in the VCR?*

Sue Buchanan is the author of several books, including *Duh-Votions* and *I'm Alive and the Doctor's Dead*. She cowrote *Friends through Thick and Thin* and *Confessions of Friends through Thick and Thin* with Gloria Gaither, Peggy Benson, and Joy MacKenzie. She lives with her husband, Wayne, in Nashville.

Phil Callaway is a popular speaker and the author of numerous bestsellers, including *Who Put the Skunk in the Trunk?* and *I Used to Have Answers, Now I Have Kids*. Visit Phil's Web site at www.philcallaway.ab.ca.

Patsy Clairmont is a featured speaker at Women of Faith

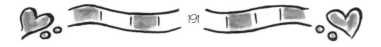

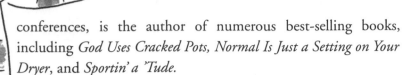

conferences, is the author of numerous best-selling books, including *God Uses Cracked Pots, Normal Is Just a Setting on Your Dryer,* and *Sportin' a 'Tude.*

G. Ron Darbee is the author of *Nothing Builds Togetherness like Wrestling for Remote Control* and *The Lord Is My Shepherd and I'm about to be Sheared!* His award-winning short stories have been published in a wide range of publications.

Susan Duke is a best-selling author, inspirational speaker, and singer. She coauthored several titles, including *Courage for the Chicken-Hearted* and *Heartlifters for Women,* as well as the God Things Come in Small Packages series, and she is the author of *Earth Angels.* She speaks in conferences, seminars, and churches nationwide.

Chris Ewing is the author of *An Owner's Guide to Fatherhood: Living with Children and Other Creatures.* He has been married for more than two decades and is the father of three children.

Barbara Johnson is the author of many best-selling books of humor and inspiration, including *Boomerang Joy* and *Stick a Geranium in Your Hat and Be Happy!* She is also a featured speaker at Women of Faith conferences.

Tina Krause is a newspaper columnist, mother, and the author of *Laughter Therapy: A Dose of Humor for the Christian Woman's Heart.*

Karen Scalf Linamen is the author of numerous books, including *Welcome to the Funny Farm* and *I'm Not Suffering from Insanity . . . I'm Enjoying Every Minute of It!* She is the author of more than one hundred magazine articles and speaks frequently at churches, women's retreats, and writers' conferences.

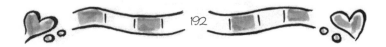

Brennan Manning is a beloved speaker and author whose titles include *The Ragamuffin Gospel, Abba's Child, The Signature of Jesus,* and *Ruthless Trust.*

Dave Meurer is the winner of numerous state and national writing awards and honors. His writings have appeared in such major publications as *Focus on the Family* and *HomeLife.* He and his family live in northern California.

Helen Widger Middlebrooke is the mother of nine and the author of *Lessons for a Super Mom: Devotions from the Middle of Life.*

Cathy Lee Phillips is a devotional speaker, retreat leader, and humorist, as well as the author of *Silver in the Slop and Other Surprises! Gutsy Little Flowers,* and *Aging, Ailments, and Attitudes.*

Rhonda Rhea is an inspirational speaker and author of *Amusing Grace: Hilarity and Hope in the Everyday Calamity of Motherhood.* The mother of five and wife of a pastor, Rhonda writes regularly for *HomeLife* magazine and *ParentLife* magazine, and her articles have appeared in *Today's Christian Woman, Christian Parenting Today,* and other publications.

Cal and Rose Samra are the authors of the best-selling *Holy Humor* and *More Holy Humor,* as well as the editors and publishers of *The Joyful Noiseletter.* They are the founders of the Fellowship of Merry Christians, an organization dedicated to helping unite Christians through the joy of the Lord.

Lowell D. Streiker, PhD, is an inspirational humorist, speaker, and author who has written, edited, and contributed to nearly thirty books. His latest are *An Encyclopedia of Humor, Nelson's Amazing Bible Trivia (Book 3), Nelson's Big Book of Laughter—A to Z, Little Book of Laughter,* and *A Treasury of*

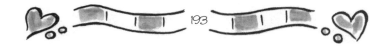

Humor. He and his wife, Connie, live in Cottonwood, California, with their three dogs, two horses, and four cats.

Luci Swindoll, who formerly served as vice-president of public relations for *Insight for Living* and as an executive with Mobil Oil Corp., is the author of numerous titles, including *I Married Adventure*. Luci is also one of the featured speakers at Women of Faith conferences.

Charles Tindell is a nursing-home chaplain and the author of *Seeing Beyond the Wrinkles: Stories of Ageless Courage, Humor, and Faith*.

Stan Toler is the senior pastor of Trinity Church of the Nazarene in Oklahoma City. He is the author of several titles, including *The Buzzards Are Circling, but God's Not Finished with Me Yet* and *God Has Never Failed Me, but He's Sure Scared Me to Death a Few Times*.

Laura Jensen Walker is a popular public speaker and author whose works include *Through the Rocky Road and into the Rainbow Sherbet* and *Love Handles for the Romantically Impaired*. She and her husband live in northern California.

Lynn Bowen Walker is a freelance writer whose work has appeared in numerous periodicals, including *Marriage Partnership, Christian Parenting Today, Moody, Glamour,* and *American Baby*. She and her husband, Mark, live in Los Gatos, California, and are the parents of two sons.

Tim Wildmon is vice president of the American Family Association, a Christian organization based in Tupelo, Mississippi. He and his wife, Alison, make their home in Saltillo, Mississippi, with their three children.

Other Great Books in the Humor for the Heart™ Series

Humor for the Heart
ISBN: *1-58229-128-4*

Humor for a Woman's Heart
ISBN: *1-58229-205-1*

Humor for a Woman's Heart 2
ISBN: *1-58229-230-2*

Humor for a Teacher's Heart
ISBN: *1-58229-394-5*

Humor for a Mom's Heart
ISBN: *1-58229-266-3*

The best-selling Humor for the Heart series has become a national favorite, and these humorous editions portray the lighter side of the joys, challenges, and adventures of living in today's world.

This series includes best-selling authors, like Patsy Clairmont, Max Lucado, Barbara Johnson, Chonda Pierce, Marilyn Meberg, Martha Bolton, Mark Lowry, and many more. The humor in these hilarious books has the power to transform a down day into an optimistic adventure or an OK day into a celebration. These books are guaranteed to lift you above the mundane and give your heart a healthy dose of optimism and hope.

Available where good books are sold.